Grappling with God

Explorations of the Old Testament
for personal and small group use

BOOK THREE

Wisdom, songs and stories

Nick Fawcett

Kevin
Mayhew

First published in 2000 by
KEVIN MAYHEW LTD
Buxhall
Stowmarket
Suffolk IP14 3BW

0 1 2 3 4 5 6 7 8 9

ISBN 1 84003 501 3
Catalogue No 1500333

Cover design by Jonathan Stroulger
Edited by Katherine Laidler
Typesetting by Louise Selfe

Printed and bound in Great Britain

To Rev Harry Mowvley,
former lecturer at Bristol Baptist College,
whose infectious love of the Old Testament brought its pages to life

About the author

Nick Fawcett was born in 1957. He studied Theology at Bristol University and Regent's Park College, Oxford. His early years of ministry were spent in Somerset and Lancashire, and from 1989 to 1996 he was Minister of Gas Green Baptist Church, Cheltenham. From November 1996 to June 1999 he served as Toc H Chaplain and Development Officer for Wales and the West of England.

He is now concentrating full time on his career as a writer, proof-reader and indexer. His books to date are *No Ordinary Man* (1997), *Prayers For All Seasons* (1998), *Are You Listening?* (1998) and *Getting It Across* (1999), all published by Kevin Mayhew. He has also written the texts for the *Best Loved Choral Melodies Choral Collection* (1999) and had four hymns chosen for inclusion in the Churches Together Millennium Hymn Book *New Start Hymns and Songs* (1999), both also published by Kevin Mayhew.

He lives with his wife, Deborah, and their two young children, Samuel and Katie, in Wellington, Somerset.

Acknowledgements

I am indebted in the writing of this book to my wife, Deborah, for her invaluable help and support; to Katherine Laidler for all the time and work she has put in to editing the manuscript; to Peter Dainty for his invariably constructive comments and criticisms; and to Kevin Mayhew Publishers for the opportunity to put this and other material into print.

Scripture quotations are taken from the New Revised Standard Version of the Bible, copyright 1989 by the Division of Christian Education of the National Council of the Churches of Christ in the USA. Used by permission. All rights reserved.

Proverbs are taken from *The Penguin Book of Proverbs* and *Collins Gem Dictionary of Quotations*. Unless otherwise stated, the source is unknown.

Contents

Introduction

Why read the Old Testament? If I had a pound for every time I've been asked that question I would be a rich man indeed. Many people feel that it is superfluous to their requirements; a confusing and sometimes disturbing book which they feel is best left unexplored. And though I believe they are mistaken, I can understand how they reach that conclusion, for there is much in the Old Testament which is difficult to come to terms with – a multitude of passages which can seem either dull, primitive or downright barbaric by Christian standards. It is often hard to reconcile the God we find there with the God we believe has been revealed to us in Jesus Christ.

Yet to abandon the Old Testament because of such difficulties is to deny oneself untold riches. Imagine Christmas or Holy Week without the great words of the prophet Isaiah: 'The people who walked in darkness have seen a great light'; 'He was wounded for our transgressions, crushed for our iniquities; upon him was the punishment that made us whole.' Imagine Good Friday without the unforgettable cry of the Psalmist: 'My God, my God, why have you forsaken me?' Imagine Pentecost without the wonderful vision of Joel: 'Your sons and daughters shall prophesy, your old men shall dream dreams, and your young men shall see visions.' Like it or not, the Christian faith has its roots firmly in the Old Testament, and it is in the light of its pages that, at least in part, the testimony of the New must be interpreted.

The Old Testament, however, has more to offer than simply words of prophecy. It records some of the most unforgettable stories ever told: Noah and the Great Flood, Esau and Jacob, Moses crossing the Red Sea, Samson and Delilah, David and Goliath, Daniel in the lions' den, Shadrach, Meshach and Abednego, Jonah and the 'whale' – and so we could go on. Here are tales which have captured the imagination of people across the centuries, and rightly so, for as well as communicating deep theological truths they also speak directly to our human condition. Time and again we can identify with the characters in question, seeing something of ourselves in each one. It is, perhaps, in the raw human emotions so often displayed and the almost brutal honesty before God that the Old Testament's greatest strength lies. So much of what we see there mirrors what we feel and experience ourselves.

Every individual will approach the complexities thrown up by the Old Testament in their own way. For me they reflect a nation's grappling with God across the centuries. From a crude awareness of God way back in the mists of time, we move inexorably forward to an ever-deepening understanding of his greatness, love and mercy, all brought together in the anticipation of the promised Messiah. Not that the coming of Jesus means our picture of God is complete, for we too must wrestle in our turn if we are to move forward in our journey of faith. God may be fully revealed in Christ, but for now we see only in part. Like his people of old, we must press on towards the kingdom he holds in store.

In this third volume we explore three strands within the Old Testament: wisdom, songs and stories. The first of these refers to the books of Job, Proverbs and Ecclesiastes, the second to the Psalms and the Song of Solomon, and the third to the book of Daniel. The material within these could hardly be more diverse. The so-called wisdom literature explores the fundamental issues of life, ranging from the down-to-earth matters covered in Proverbs, to the great mysteries of human existence tackled by Job and Ecclesiastes. Here are some of the most distinctive books of the Old Testament, their startling honesty often coming as a shock to the unsuspecting reader. Yet there are many who, on reflection, find this very frankness to be of enormous encouragement, the books echoing and/or answering many of the questions they find themselves asking. The same could be said of the Song of Solomon, though in a different context. Perhaps the most neg-lected of all Old Testament writings, it explores, again with disarming frankness, one simple theme: the courtship of a man and woman. Moving to the Psalms, the parallels and contrasts continue. Again we find examples here of an almost brutal honesty, but equally there are passages in complete contrast exploring a host of different themes, as is fitting for a collection of songs which would regularly have been used in public worship. Finally, the book of Daniel takes us to a completely different plane, the realm of Old Testament apocalyptic. Written at a time of intense persecution, its aim was both to encourage and inspire. Examples of faithfulness triumphing over the odds, coupled with revelations of God's sovereign purpose through dreams and visions, offered hope to a nation close to despair; the assurance that good will finally emerge victorious.

Each of the volumes in this collection is designed both for individual and group use. You may find them helpful in your personal devotions, or equally they may provide material for a Bible study or house group. The themed 'chapters' have been set out with both ends in mind. They begin with an introductory paragraph which sets the scene for what follows. A scriptural reading then leads into a meditation, exploring the incidents related from the perspective of the principal character involved. The remaining sections are all designed to aid further reflection. First, a selection of proverbs related to what has gone before is offered as food for thought. The relevance of some of these will be obvious, of others less so, but make time to consider their truth or otherwise.

What does each one have to say about the subject? Do they aid understanding or confuse the issue? Do they sum up the key theme or point
in an altogether different direction? This leads on to questions for discus-
sion or personal reflection. There is no right or wrong answer to many
of these questions; rather they are designed to help apply what the
Bible has to say to our own lives. Don't rush through them with a cur-
sory 'yes' or 'no'; ask yourself what each one is driving at and whether
perhaps some have a challenge for you. Finally, additional passages of
Scripture are recommended which may help you consider further the
issues which have been raised; issues which are summed up in a con-
cluding prayer.

The meditations in this book inevitably just skim the surface of the
great wealth of material within the Old Testament. Though almost all
of the books and the key characters within them are briefly covered,
much you may consider important may find no mention. Similarly, it
is impossible in a collection such as this to explore all the theological
issues raised by the biblical passages referred to. My intention, rather,
is to make the reader feel part of the incidents related and to draw out
certain truths from these. Necessarily many questions will be left
unanswered, but if anything in the pages which follow brings home
the challenge of the Old Testament for today then I believe I will have
been true to the overriding intention of all Scripture. It is my hope that
through this collection of readings, prayers and meditations, familiar and
not so familiar stories will come alive in new and unexpected ways.

Nick Fawcett

Opening prayer

Living God,
    there comes a time for us all
    when we must meet your challenge and respond –
    a time when, try as we might,
    we can no longer go on running from your presence.
The experience can be painful and disturbing –
    facing ourselves as we really are,
    looking into the darker recesses of our minds,
    and measuring all this against your infinite goodness.
We prefer to stifle the voice of conscience,
    to avoid the uncomfortable
    and deny what we would rather not accept,
    but until we make our peace with you
    we can find no rest for our souls.
Give us, then, the courage
    to wrestle with you in the wilderness
    until our doubts are resolved,
    our reservations overcome
    and our sins dealt with.
So may we experience for ourselves
    the blessings which you alone can give.
In the name of Christ.
Amen.

*There is nothing patent in the New Testament
that is not latent in the Old.*
(Anon)

1 The mystery of suffering _____

_____ *Job*

The other day I found an old sermon which I'd preached in my teens while still cutting my teeth as a trainee for the ministry. Its theme was the problem of suffering, and the contents made me squirm with embarrassment! How could I have even begun at such a tender age to tackle one of the great mysteries of the Christian life; one which has perplexed individual believers and great theologians alike across the centuries? It is all too easy to come up with pat answers and trite assumptions which serve only to confuse the issue and add to the misery of those wrestling with inexplicable suffering. The book of Job was written precisely to counter such simplistic responses, flatly contradicting the received wisdom of his day that suffering was God's punishment for sin and that a godly life goes hand in hand with health, happiness and prosperity. There is, however, no alternative theory offered in its place. To have done that would have been to risk repeating the mistake. What Job offers instead is the ultimate conviction that even when we cannot begin to understand, and even when life flies in the face of all we believe, God is there.

Reading – Job 23:2-17

Today also my complaint is bitter;
his hand is heavy despite my groaning.
Oh, that I knew where I might find him,
that I might come even to his dwelling!
I would lay my case before him,
and fill my mouth with arguments.
I would learn what he would answer me,
and understand what he would say to me.
Would he contend with me in the greatness of his power?
No; but he would give heed to me.
There an upright person could reason with him,
and I should be acquitted for ever by my judge.

If I go forward, he is not there;
or backward, I cannot perceive him;
on the left he hides, and I cannot behold him;

I turn to the right, but I cannot see him.
But he knows the way that I take;
when he has tested me, I shall come out like gold.
My foot has held fast to his steps;
I have kept his way and have not turned aside.
I have not departed from the commandment of his lips;
I have treasured in my bosom the words of his mouth.
But he stands alone and who can dissuade him?
What he desires, that he does.
For he will complete what he appoints for me;
and many such things are in his mind.
Therefore I am terrified at his presence;
when I consider, I am in dread of him.
God has made my heart faint;
the Almighty has terrified me.
If only I could vanish in darkness,
and thick darkness would cover my face!

Meditation

What did I do wrong, can you tell me?
What terrible crime did I commit to deserve such pain,
    such sorrow,
    such suffering?
I've asked myself that day after day,
    year after year –
    the question always there,
    adding yet more torment to my private hell –
    and it's with me still,
    refusing to be silenced
    despite my every attempt to lance its poison.
Yet for all my searching I find no answer,
    no one moment of madness
    to explain these endless months of misery.
Oh, I've made my mistakes like anyone else –
    foolish words,
    foolish thoughts,
    foolish deeds –
    but nothing especially shocking,
    no worse than anything others do all around me,
    so why is it that I suffer and they don't,
    I endure such agony and they enjoy such blessing?
It makes no sense, for I've tried to be faithful,

day after day seeking the Lord's will,
studying his word,
following his commandments,
so why does he hide his face from me
in my hour of despair?
Repent, that's what they tell me,
acknowledge my weakness,
confess my mistakes,
and all shall be well.
They mean well, I know that,
each one, in their own way,
trying to make sense of the inexplicable,
but if they only knew the added pain they cause me,
the extra burden they impose,
perhaps then, like me, they'd learn to be silent,
accepting that the ways of God are beyond us all.
I don't blame them, for they want answers,
easy solutions to uncomfortable questions,
but you can take it from me –
from someone who's experienced
depths of suffering I pray you'll never know –
it's not that simple,
not that simple at all.

To ponder

- The gem cannot be polished without friction, nor man be perfected without trials. (Chinese proverb)
- Pain is the price that God puts on all things.
- Who suffers much is silent.
- Each cross bears its own inscription.

To discuss

- What situations of suffering in the world today do you find it hard to make sense of?
- Have you ever been offered well-intentioned advice in times of suffering which has served to hurt rather than help? What was it?
- How would you respond to someone in a similar situation?

To consider further

Read John 9:1-12. Jesus here counters the idea that sin has anything to do with suffering. Are there still times today, however, when we hear a 'success gospel' being preached, promising automatic blessing as a result of faithfulness?

Prayer

Living God,
    there is so much suffering in this world of ours;
    so much pain, so much sorrow, so much evil.
It is hard sometimes to reconcile all this
    with it being your world too,
    created by you and precious in your sight.
We search desperately for answers,
    clinging first to this and then to that,
    and underneath there are times
    when our faith begins to crumble.
Teach us, though we cannot always see it,
    that you are there,
    sharing in our anguish,
    carrying in yourself the agony of creation
    as it groans under the weight of imperfection.
Teach us that you will not rest
    until that day when all suffering is ended,
    when evil is no more
    and your kingdom is established;
    and in that assurance give us strength to face each day,
    whatever it might bring.
Amen.

2 Light in our darkness

Job

While the book of Job does not offer an answer to the problem of suffering, this does not mean it is devoid of hope. On the contrary, despite everything he experiences, Job ultimately finds his faith deepened and his awareness of God enriched. The journey was undeniably painful, but there can be no doubt that he emerges stronger and wiser for it. And there are many, having wrestled with deep suffering themselves, who can testify to something similar. Not that any welcomed what they faced, still less that they saw it as inflicted by God, but rather the experience leads them on to deeper insights into the ultimate realities of life. The mystery is not fully resolved, yet some sense is made of it: out of darkness God brings light; out of evil, something good; out of despair, hope. To me this is one of the great lessons of this unforgettable book.

Reading – Job 29:1-6; 30:16-23

Job again took up his discourse and said:
'O that I were as in the months of old,
as in the days when God watched over me;
when his lamp shone over my head,
and by his light I walked through darkness;
when I was in my prime,
when the friendship of God was upon my tent;
when the Almighty was still with me,
when my children were around me;
when my steps were washed with milk,
and the rock poured out for me streams of oil!

Now my soul is poured out within me;
days of affliction have taken hold of me.
The night racks my bones,
and the pain that gnaws me takes no rest.
With violence he seizes my garment;
he grasps me by the collar of my tunic.
He has cast me down into the mire,
and I have become like dust and ashes.
I cry to you and you do not answer me;

I stand, and you merely look at me.
You have turned cruel to me;
with the might of your hand you persecute me.
You lift me up on the wind, make me ride on it,
and you toss me about in the roar of the storm.
I know that you will bring me to death,
and to the house appointed for all the living.

Meditation

I used to laugh once, long ago,
    life overflowing with happiness,
    brimful with joy.
You find that hard to believe?
I'm not surprised,
    for to see me now –
    the lines of misery on my forehead,
    the despair deep in my eyes –
    you'd think I must have known only sorrow,
    a lifetime of perpetual shadow and endless pain.
Yet it wasn't always like that, not by a long way.
There was a time when my spirit soared and my heart skipped,
    when the sun rose rich with promise, new every morning,
    each day a priceless treasure,
    each moment a gift to be savoured.
I rejoiced then in the beauty of it all,
    overwhelmed by the wonder of creation
    and the sweetness of life,
    and I lifted my voice to God in exultation,
    his praise always on my lips.
Only that was then, and this is now,
    such carefree moments a distant memory,
    troubling my thoughts like some half-remembered dream,
    so that I question if they ever truly were.
Yet it's no good looking back;
    no answers to be found there.
It's the future that matters,
    and despite all I've faced I await it with confidence,
    convinced that God will be with me to lead me forward;
    for, believe it or not, through all the pain and heartache
    somehow I've grown,

my faith stronger,
refined through fire,
able to withstand whatever may be thrown against it.
I may not celebrate quite as I used to,
for I will bear the scars within me until my dying day,
but I will laugh with a greater understanding,
I will love with a deeper passion,
and I will live with a richer sense of purpose,
for I have stared into the darkness,
a blackness beyond words,
and I've found God coming to meet me,
his light reaching out, even there!

Reading – Job 38:1-2; 40:7-9; 42:1-6

Then the Lord answered Job out of the whirlwind: 'Who is this that darkens counsel by words without knowledge? . . . Gird up your loins like a man: I will question you, and you declare to me. Will you even put me in the wrong? Will you condemn me that you may be justified? Have you an arm like God, and can you thunder with a voice like his?'

Then Job answered the Lord: 'I know that you can do all things, and that no purpose of yours can be thwarted. "Who is this that hides counsel without knowledge?" Therefore I have uttered what I did not understand, things too wonderful for me, which I did not know. "Hear, and I will speak; I will question you, and you declare to me." I had heard of you by the hearing of the ear, but now my eye sees you; therefore I despise myself, and repent in dust and ashes.'

To ponder

- Joy and sorrow are next-door neighbours.
- It is misery enough to have once been happy.
- Bitter pills may have blessed effects.
- Suffering is bitter, but its fruits are sweet.
- If there were no clouds, we should not enjoy the sun.
- Through hardship to the stars.

To discuss

- Have you come through difficult times the stronger for them? In what way?
- What did you find most helpful during your experiences? From whom or what did you draw most strength?
- How far is it possible to have pleasure without pain?

To consider further

Read Matthew 26:36-46, 27:45-46 and 28:1-10. Take heart from the assurance these verses bring that darkness can never finally overcome the light.

Prayer

Gracious God,
    you came to our world through Jesus Christ,
    and despite everything that conspires against you,
    your love continues to shine through him.
You conquered the forces of evil,
    you overcame the sting of death,
    and you brought joy out of sorrow,
    hope out of despair.
Teach us, whatever we may face,
    to hold on to that truth,
    confident that you will always lead us out of darkness
    into your marvellous light.
Hold on to us when life is hard,
    and assure us that you are present
    even in the bleakest moments,
    able to use every moment of each day
    in ways beyond our imagining.
Amen.

3 Stewards of creation

David

Which of us hasn't at some time gazed up at the night sky and been overwhelmed by a sense of our insignificance in terms of the enormity of space? It is hard to believe, faced with the scale of that contrast, that our lives can ultimately be of any consequence beyond our immediate circle of family and friends. Any claims to the contrary are surely a naïve delusion. It is thoughts such as these which lie behind the words of David in Psalm 8, but the conclusions he reaches are very different. Hard to believe it may be, but each one of us, he argues, holds a unique place in God's creation and a special responsibility for it. Today, with growing pressures on our environment and the very real threat of global warming, the words of this Psalm take on particular significance. We have plundered this world's resources too freely, with little thought for our long-term responsibilities. As Christians we need to add our voice to the mounting calls for a sensible stewarding of creation. To fail in that is to betray the trust God has placed in our hands.

Reading – Psalm 8

O Lord, our Sovereign,
how majestic is your name in all the earth!

You have set your glory above the heavens.
Out of the mouths of babes and infants
you have founded a bulwark because of your foes,
to silence the enemy and the avenger.

When I look at your heavens, the work of your fingers,
the moon and the stars that you have established;
what are human beings that you are mindful of them,
mortals that you care for them?

Yet you have made them a little lower than God,
and crowned them with glory and honour.
You have given them dominion over the works of your hands;
you have put all things under their feet,
all sheep and oxen,

and also the beasts of the field,
the birds of the air, and the fish of the sea,
whatever passes along the paths of the seas.

O Lord, our Sovereign,
how majestic is your name in all the earth!

Meditation

Is it possible?
Can it really be true that God has time for you and me?
It seems preposterous,
  stretching credulity to the limit,
  for what place can we have in the grand scheme of things;
  what reason for God to concern himself about our fate?
I look at the vastness of the heavens
  and the awesome tapestry of creation,
  and we're nothing,
  just the tiniest speck against the great backdrop of history.
And yet amazingly,
  astonishingly,
  we matter!
Not just *noticed* by God,
  but *precious* to him,
  special,
  unique,
  holding an unrivalled place in his affections and purpose.
Can it be true? –
  a little lower than God himself,
  made in his image?
It sounds fantastic,
  almost blasphemous,
  for who are we –
  weak, sinful, fatally flawed humanity –
  to be likened to the sovereign God,
  creator of the ends of the earth,
  enthroned in splendour,
  perfect in his holiness?
Yet there it is,
  incredible yet true,
  not just part of creation but stewards over it –

the beasts of the field,
the birds of the air,
the fish of the sea –
their future in our hands;
this wonderful world,
so beautiful,
so fragile,
placed into our keeping,
held on trust.
That's how much he loves us,
the ultimate proof of his care.
What a wonderful privilege!
What an awesome responsibility!

To ponder

- Marvels are many, but man is the greatest. *(Antigone)*
- Remember you are but a man.

To discuss

- Is there a united Church voice on environmental issues? Do Christians make themselves sufficiently heard on such matters?
- What can we do individually to demonstrate our commitment to the environment? Do we do it? Are such steps sufficient, or is more needed?
- Modern technology is taking us into uncharted waters – genetic engineering, for example. It is easy to offer a knee-jerk reaction to such developments, but what are the theological implications of such research? Discuss both the potential benefits and the dangers.

To consider further

Read Revelation 21:1. Is there a danger of Christians abandoning their responsibilities in this world through focusing too much on the next?

Prayer

Lord of all,
    your love for us involves responsibility
    as well as privilege.
Our place in creation carries a duty to nurture
    rather than simply exploit it.
Forgive us for our part in a society
    that has too often lived for today
    with no thought of tomorrow,
    plundering this world's resources
    with little care as to the consequences.
Challenge the hearts and minds of people everywhere,
    that they and we may understand more fully
    both the wonder and the fragility
    of this planet you have given us,
    and so honour our calling to be faithful stewards of it all.
In the name of Christ we pray.
Amen.

4 Counting our blessings

David

Just occasionally in life something happens to remind us of the special things we need to celebrate, those blessings, those gifts which really matter. Sadly such moments are all too rare. More often than not we lurch from one demand, one crisis, one responsibility to another, scarcely finding time to draw breath and reflect on the reasons we have to give thanks. We find ourselves complaining of our lot, resenting the pressures put upon us, viewing life from a distorted angle and jaundiced perspective. It is a vicious circle which feeds on itself – the more sorry for ourselves we feel, the more cause there seems for such feelings. Yet if we stop and truly consider – if we make time, in the words of the old hymn, to 'count our blessings' – life seems very different. There is so much that is not only good but indescribably wonderful, beautiful beyond words. Make time in your life to consider such things and you may well find yourself echoing the words of David repeated below: 'The boundary lines have fallen for me in pleasant places; I have a goodly heritage'.

Reading – Psalm 16

Protect me, O God, for in you I take refuge.
I say to the Lord, 'You are my Lord;
I have no good apart from you.'
As for the holy ones in the land, they are the noble,
in whom is all my delight.

Those who choose another god multiply their sorrows;
their drink offerings of blood I will not pour out
or take their names upon my lips.

The Lord is my chosen portion and my cup;
you hold my lot.
The boundary lines have fallen for me in pleasant places;
I have a goodly heritage.

I bless the Lord who gives me counsel;
in the night also my heart instructs me.
I keep the Lord always before me;
because he is at my right hand, I shall not be moved.

Therefore my heart is glad, and my soul rejoices;
my body also rests secure.
For you do not give me up to Sheol,
or let your faithful one see the Pit.

You show me the path of life.
In your presence there is fullness of joy;
in your right hand are pleasures for evermore.

Meditation

I'm a lucky man –
 so much to be thankful for,
 so much to celebrate,
 my life running over with good things!
All right, I've not got everything, admittedly,
 and yes, perhaps I would change the odd detail
 given the chance,
 but nothing major,
 certainly nothing to fret over,
 for when I stop to count my blessings,
 weigh things up in the balance,
 I realise how truly fortunate I am.
I should never have forgotten, of course,
 but I did,
 and I do,
 time after time,
 to my shame not only failing to be thankful
 but actually complaining,
 bemoaning my lot,
 dwelling on the bad rather than the good.
It's crazy, I know,
 but we all do it, don't we? –
 so much taken for granted,
 unrecognised,
 unappreciated;

so feeble a response to so vast a treasure.
Probably it will always be the same,
   despite my best intentions,
   the gratitude I feel now
   evaporating yet again before I know it.
Probably I'll still end up feeling sorry for myself,
   looking enviously at my neighbour,
   muttering that life's not fair.
But today at least I want to give thanks,
   I want to celebrate everything in life that is good and special,
   and, above all, I want to praise God,
   to whom I owe it all.

To ponder

- Familiarity breeds contempt.
- Goods that are much on show lose their colour. *(Brazilian proverb)*
- When you drink from the stream, remember the spring. *(Chinese proverb)*
- Gratitude is the least of virtues, but ingratitude is the worst of vices.
- Much of what we see depends on what we are looking for.

To discuss

- How often do we make time to thank God for all he has given? Why is it that we so easily take things for granted?
- What do you think is the best way of expressing our gratitude to God?
- Do we show our thanks to others as often as we should do? If not, why is that? Why is expressing our appreciation important?

To consider

Read Philippians 4:4-7. Make a list of all the reasons you have to be happy. Count your blessings, literally – then give thanks for them.

Prayer

Lord,
    we have so much to thank you for,
    yet all too often we take it for granted.
Instead of counting our blessings,
    we dwell on our problems.
Instead of celebrating all you have given,
    we brood about what we might yet have.
In our pursuit of illusory dreams of happiness
    we lose sight of the gifts each day brings,
    the countless reasons we have to rejoice.
Forgive us for forgetting how fortunate we are,
    and help us to appreciate the wonder
    of all we have received from your loving hands.
In the name of Christ.
Amen.

5 The dark night of the soul _____

_____ *David*

The opening words of the twenty-second Psalm must surely be some of the most familiar in all Scripture. Most likely, however, we recognise them not as part of this Psalm, but as the anguished cry of Jesus from the cross. It is inevitable that we will interpret the words in this light, the association imbuing them with special meaning, but we should never forget that centuries before this they were uttered in another poignant cry of dereliction. Just what lay behind them we shall never know, but it is clear that something happened to David to bring him to the depths of despair. Life, it seems, had lost its meaning for him. So it has been across the years for countless others; an unseen multitude who, their lives already in turmoil, have endured the added anguish of even God seeming to be absent. No one would wish such moments on anybody, but we should take heart that even those closest to God can experience such testing moments, and more heart still from the fact that very often it has been precisely during those times that God has been supremely at work.

Reading – Psalm 22:1-2, 7-11, 16b-19, 23-24

My God, my God, why have you forsaken me?
Why are you so far from helping me,
from the words of my groaning?
O my God, I cry by day, but you do not answer;
and by night, but find no rest.

All who see me mock at me;
they make mouths at me, they shake their heads;
'Commit your cause to the Lord; let him deliver –
let him rescue the one in whom he delights!'

Yet it was you who took me from the womb,
you who kept me safe on my mother's breast.
On you I was cast from my birth,
and since my mother bore me you have been my God.
Do not be far from me,
for trouble is near
and there is no one to help.

A company of evildoers encircles me.
My hands and feet have shrivelled;
I can count all my bones.
They stare and gloat over me;
they divide my clothes among themselves,
and for my clothing they cast lots.

But you, O Lord, do not be far away!
O my help, come quickly to my aid!

You who fear the Lord, praise him!
All you offspring of Jacob, glorify him;
stand in awe of him, all you offspring of Israel!
For he did not despise or abhor
the affliction of the afflicted;
he did not hide his face from me,
but heard when I cried to him.

Meditation

I felt alone,
    utterly abandoned,
    not just by man but by God,
    and I was bereft,
    desolate,
    broken in body, mind and spirit.
How could it be happening, I asked myself?
Why had God brought me thus far,
    always by my side,
    always there to guide me,
    only to desert me when I needed him most?
It made no sense,
    faith itself thrown into turmoil,
    for it denied everything:
    the love, the purpose, the mercy I'd trusted in so long.
Yet when I cried out in agony of spirit,
    there was nothing –
    not a word,
    not a sign –
    nothing;
    and it was crushing,
    the bleakest, blackest moment of my life.

I wanted to let go,
> give up,
> for surely anything, even the oblivion of death,
> was preferable to this.

Yet somehow I held on.
Despite the emptiness,
> the awful silence,
> I kept praying,
> remembering all that God had done.

And somewhere, deep within, hope flickered again,
> spluttering,
> tremulous,
> like a smouldering candle,
> a flame caught in the breeze,
> yet alight once more,
> refusing to be extinguished.

It took time, mind you, before the cloud lifted;
> not just days, but weeks, months –
> a long and lonely struggle in the wilderness –
> and I often wondered if I would ever taste joy again,
> my heart dance once more to the familiar tunes of old.

I was wrong, of course,
> for I came through finally,
> stronger and tougher through the experience.

God hadn't forsaken me;
> he'd been there all along,
> right there in the darkness
> sharing my sorrow,
> bearing my pain.

But for a time I'd believed him lost to me,
> I'd glimpsed the agony of separation,
> and it was more terrible than you can imagine.

God save anyone from facing that again.

To ponder

- The wound that bleeds inwardly is most dangerous.
- Small sorrows speak; great ones are silent.
- Sadness and gladness succeed each other.
- All the darkness in the world cannot put out the light of one candle.
  (*Tubby Clayton*)

To discuss

- Have you ever felt far from God? How did you cope during that time? What did you find most and least helpful?
- With the benefit of hindsight, can you identify times in your life when God was at work even though you were totally unaware of it? What were they?
- How would you respond to someone going through the 'dark night of the soul'? What help or encouragement would you try to offer?

To consider further

Read Matthew 27:45-50. What does the fact that Jesus felt abandoned by God and cut off from him say to you? What lessons can we draw from it?

Prayer

Gracious God,
    there are times when life seems dark
    and your purpose hard to fathom;
    when try as we might to make sense of it,
    so much is impossible to understand.
We call to you but you do not seem to answer,
    we seek your presence but feel utterly alone.
Help us, when such moments strike,
    to remember all the ways you have been with us
    and the guidance you have given.
Help us to recall the coming of your light into the world,
    and the promise that nothing shall ever overcome it.
Gracious God, when we lose hold of you,
    keep hold of us and see us safely through,
    in the name of Jesus Christ,
    the crucified yet risen Lord.
Amen.

6 Shepherd of the sheep _____

_____ *David*

I thought long and hard before writing this meditation based on the twenty-third Psalm. What can I or anyone else add to these wonderful words which have brought such comfort and inspiration to so many across the centuries. The answer, of course, is nothing. Here is a psalm with a timeless quality that has a power to move people as few words can even begin to; a psalm which touches us at some deep subconscious level, speaking to our innermost needs. But as I reflected on all this, I was suddenly struck by the fact that David himself had, of course, in his youth been a shepherd. That in itself seemed an observation worth exploring. When he wrote 'The Lord is my shepherd', he knew what he was talking about, the words rich with personal associations. Here was no sentimental comparison. It was rather the testimony of someone who understood the commitment and devotion shepherding requires, and who in an outpouring of wonder realised that here was an illustration of the astonishing love God has for us and all his people.

Reading – Psalm 23

The Lord is my shepherd, I shall not want.
He makes me lie down in green pastures;
he leads me beside still waters;
he restores my soul.
He leads me in right paths for his name's sake.

Even though I walk through the darkest valley,
I fear no evil;
for you are with me;
your rod and your staff –
they comfort me.

You prepare a table before me
in the presence of my enemies;
you anoint my head with oil;
my cup overflows.
Surely goodness and mercy shall follow me

all the days of my life,
and I shall dwell in the house of the Lord
my whole life long.

Meditation

I met him out on the hills,
    night drawing in,
    the wind, chill –
    a solitary shepherd,
    brow furrowed,
    searching for a sheep gone astray.
And suddenly it all came flooding back,
    those long hours I had spent as a boy
    out in the fields tending my father's flock.
Good days, on the whole –
    time to think,
    to pray,
    or simply to enjoy the beauty of this world God has given.
But demanding also,
    even dangerous sometimes –
    out in the fiercest of storms,
    harassed by wild beasts,
    keeping watch through the lonely hours of the night.
Funny really, isn't it? –
    all that over a bunch of sheep,
    for let's face it, they're stupid creatures at the best of times,
    often driving you to near distraction.
You try to help them and what do they do? –
    wander away as soon as look at you.
You try to protect them,
    but, half a chance, and they're off again,
    straight into the teeth of danger.
Infuriating!
Yet somehow a bond develops between you,
    until the time comes when, if you're worth your salt,
    you'll do anything for those sheep,
    even risk your own life to save their necks.
You think that strange?
You shouldn't,
    for we're like sheep ourselves,
    as foolish, headstrong and maddening as any of them –

following the crowd,
ignoring guidance,
careering blindly towards catastrophe.
Why should anyone bother with us?
And yet the Lord does just that,
like a shepherd,
always there to guard us, guide us, feed us,
seeking when we're lost,
rejoicing when we're found,
protecting us from evil,
meeting our every need.
Would he risk his life for us, as I for my sheep?
It sounds ridiculous, I know,
too fanciful for words,
and yet when I consider the extent of his love,
the care he shows each day,
I really believe that he would;
that not only would he risk his life
but, if necessary, he'd give it, freely and gladly,
willing to die for us so that we might live!

To ponder

- Love covers many infirmities.
- To be beloved is above all bargains.
- Where love is, there is faith.
- Love is without reason.

To discuss

- What do you find most moving about Psalm 23? Which parts of it speak most powerfully to you?
- What do you understand by 'green pastures' and 'still waters'? In what ways have you been conscious of God leading you towards these?
- What qualities of a shepherd do you find most encouraging in terms of God's dealing with us?

To consider further

Read John 10:1-18. What do these words of Jesus add to Psalm 23?

Prayer

Loving God,
    time and again we have gone astray from you.
You seek us out,
    you set us on our feet,
    and we believe next time it will be different,
    but it's not;
    still we wander from your side.
We are weak and foolish,
    undeserving of your love,
    yet still you reach out to us,
    drawing us back to your side.
We praise you for the wonder of your grace,
    for your willingness through Christ
    to lay down your life for the life of the world.
We thank you for your constant provision of all our needs.
Have mercy on our repeated failures,
    and continue to guide us, we pray,
    watching over us even when we lose sight of you.
Lead us on through the changes and chances of this life,
    and through the valley of the shadow of death,
    until we are safely gathered into your kingdom
    and the journey is done.
In the name of the shepherd of all,
    Jesus Christ our Lord.
Amen.

7 Living with failure _____

_____ _David_

The words of the Psalms never fail to astound me. Written over three thousand years ago, they are able to speak today as if the words were fresh on the page. None more so than Psalm 51. Its cry of frustration is one which finds echoes in the experience of every Christian believer, reminiscent of the anguished cry of the Apostle Paul: 'Wretched man that I am! Who will rescue me from this body of death?' (Romans 7:24). Time and again we attempt to amend our ways, to conquer a particular failing, to follow Christ more closely, to live more faithfully as his disciples. Yet time and again the story is the same, the old weaknesses rear their ugly head and we find ourselves back where we started. The fact is we cannot change ourselves, however much we may wish to; we are dependent upon the grace of God and his transforming power at work within us. That truth may be self-evident to us today in the light of Jesus; the wonder of this psalm is that David recognised it well over a thousand years before Christ's coming!

Reading – Psalm 51:1-12

Have mercy on me, O God,
according to your steadfast love;
according to your abundant mercy
blot out my transgressions.
Wash me thoroughly from my iniquity,
and cleanse me from my sin.

For I know my transgressions,
and my sin is ever before me.
Against you, you alone, have I sinned,
and done what is evil in your sight,
so that you are justified in your sentence
and blameless when you pass judgement.
Indeed, I was born guilty,
a sinner when my mother conceived me.

You desire truth in the inward being;
therefore teach me wisdom in my secret heart.

Purge me with hyssop, and I shall be clean;
wash me, and I shall be whiter than snow.
Let me hear joy and gladness;
let the bones that you have crushed rejoice.
Hide your face from my sins,
and blot out all my iniquities.

Create in me a clean heart, O God,
and put a new and right spirit within me.
Do not cast me away from your presence,
and do not take your holy spirit from me.
Restore to me the joy of your salvation,
and sustain in me a willing heart.

Meditation

What can I say, Lord?
What *can* I say?
I've failed you again, haven't I?
Despite all my promises,
    all my good intentions,
    I've gone and let you down
    like so many times before.
And I'm sickened,
    crushed,
    disgusted with myself,
    ashamed I could be so pathetically weak,
    so hopelessly false.
I tried so hard, that's what gets me down.
I was determined to make up for the lapses of the past,
    to show you that I'm really serious
    about this business of discipleship,
    and to prove that the trust you've shown in me,
    your willingness to forgive and go on forgiving,
    actually means something to me,
    despite the way it may seem.
But could I do it?
No.
For a few hours,
    a few days, perhaps,
    but finally I fell as I always do,
    back into the old familiar ways.

Why, Lord?
What's wrong with me?
What am I going to do?
I can't change,
    not by myself.
I've tried it,
    and it's just no good,
    the weaknesses running too deep,
    too much a part of me,
    for me to conquer them alone.
It's in your hands, Lord,
    only you have the power to help me.
I know I don't deserve it,
    that I've no claim on your love or mercy,
    but I'm begging you,
    pleading on bended knee,
    pardon my iniquities.
Deal kindly, despite my folly,
    cleanse my heart and renew my spirit.
Mould me,
    fashion me,
    forgive me,
    restore me,
    so that perhaps one day, by your grace,
    I may serve as I should.
Lord, in your mercy, hear my prayer.

To ponder

- Mischief comes without calling for.
- Sin is the root of sorrow. *(Chinese proverb)*
- Past shame, past grace.
- If your heart is in your prayer, God will know it.

To discuss

- What do you think is the key to true repentance? Does verse 17 give us a clue? Though we are finally dependent on God's grace, do you think we have a part to play in securing God's forgiveness? If so, what is it?

- Can there be genuine repentance without first acknowledging our mistakes to ourselves? Do we make time for this, or simply generalise about our faults? Are we sufficiently honest with ourselves?
- Many Christians, despite the promise of God's mercy, still find it hard to believe themselves truly forgiven. What sort of reasons might there be for us finding it hard to accept the reality of God's pardon?

To consider further

Read 1 John 1:5-10. We may acknowledge our faults before God, but are we willing to do the same before others? Is this the real test of our sincerity? Can there be one without the other?

Prayer

Lord,
　　it is easy to go through the motions of confession;
　　to claim we are sorry for our sin
　　and to make promises about our desire to serve you
　　without really thinking about what we are saying.
Familiarity leads us to take your grace for granted,
　　and so we fail to appreciate
　　the gravity of letting you down.
Yet though your nature is always to have mercy,
　　you are grieved by our failings,
　　not least because they deny us the fullness of life
　　which you desire for all your people.
Help us, then, to see ourselves as we really are,
　　the bad as well as the good,
　　and give us a genuine sense of repentance
　　over everything in our lives that is contrary to your will.
So may we receive the forgiveness you long to give,
　　and experience your transforming, renewing power,
　　through the grace of our Lord Jesus Christ.
Amen.

8 Time's paces

Moses

There can be few of us who haven't at some point felt sobered by the ephemerality of life. Most of the time we succeed in pushing thoughts of this kind to the back of our minds, but occasionally they force their way back into our consciousness, refusing to be silenced. Psalm 90 – fascinatingly, attributed to Moses – deals with such disturbing matters with a frank, almost brutal, honesty. Like it or not, we are told, life is passing and nothing can halt its progress. It would be easy to move from here to a maudlin self-pity, but instead the psalmist turns to focus on God whose eternal nature stands in such contrast to our own transience. He alone holds the future, just as he has held the past; such human concepts scarcely applicable in the divine context. Yet it is not these with which this Psalm is finally concerned so much as the present, a present which all too often is marred by the fact and consequences of human sinfulness. If this short span of ours on earth is not to be wasted, we need God's grace to help us, to set us free from the self-imposed chains which bind us. That is as true today as it has ever been.

Reading – Psalm 90

Lord, you have been our dwelling place in all the generations.
Before the mountains were brought forth,
or ever you had formed the earth and the world,
from everlasting to everlasting you are God.

You turn us back to dust,
and say, 'Turn back you mortals.'
For a thousand years in your sight
are like yesterday when it is past,
or like a watch in the night.

You sweep them away; they are like a dream,
like grass that is renewed in the morning;
in the morning it flourishes and is renewed;
in the evening it fades and withers.

For we are consumed by your anger;
by your wrath we are overwhelmed.
You have set our iniquities before you,
our secret sins in the light of your countenance.

For all our days pass away under your wrath;
our years come to an end like a sigh.
The days of our life are seventy years,
or perhaps eighty, if we are strong;
even then their span is only toil and trouble;
they are soon gone, and we fly away.

Who considers the power of your anger?
Your wrath is as great as the fear that is due you.
So teach us to count our days
that we may gain a wise heart.

Turn, O Lord! How long?
Have compassion on your servants!
Satisfy us in the morning with your steadfast love,
so that we may rejoice and be glad all our days.
Make us glad as many days as you have afflicted us,
and as many years as we have seen evil.
Let your work be manifest to your servants,
and your glorious power to their children.
Let the favour of the Lord our God be upon us
and prosper for us the work of our hands –
O prosper the work of our hands!

Meditation

I had a shock today.
I caught sight of my reflection in a pool of water,
    and I didn't recognise the man I saw there.
He looked old,
    anxious,
    weary,
    the hair thinning and flecked with grey,
    the forehead pitted with wrinkles,
    the eyes heavy, full of trouble,
    as though he bore the cares of the world on his shoulders,
    and I thought, 'What a shame . . . poor old fellow . . .
    who's he?'
Only, of course, it was me,
    those worn and jaded features
    reflecting the man I'd become,
    and I was overwhelmed suddenly
    by an awareness of my mortality,
    the fleeting nature of this brief span of ours,
    here today and gone tomorrow.

Yes, I knew it before, in theory anyway,
    but today it's hit home with a chilling intensity –
    the stark realisation that life is rushing by
    and nothing can stop it;
    that all our hopes and plans, toiling and striving,
    finally come to nothing.
It's not a pleasant thought, is it?
Yet funnily enough I can live with that, just about,
    for I know that though I may change, God does not,
    his power, his purpose, always the same.
It's not the fact of death that troubles me,
    so much as the waste of life,
    the way we fritter away the days God has given,
    each one poisoned by our folly and sinfulness.
We all do it,
    a thoughtless act here,
    a selfish deed there,
    and before we know it the ripples are everywhere,
    a multitude of lives caught in their wash –
    so surprising a result from so little a splash.
There's no escape, not by ourselves –
    we're all trapped in this vicious vortex of destruction,
    and only God can set us free.
We've no right to expect it –
    his judgement is well-deserved –
    but if we ask in true humility,
    if we acknowledge our faults
    and throw ourselves upon his grace,
    he may yet hear our prayer and have mercy.
Remember that, my friend,
    while there's still time and life beckons,
    for, though we can't change the future,
    with God's help we can still shape the present.
Turn to him, and the years we are given may yet bring us joy,
    our toil and trouble forgotten,
    gladness to last us all our days.

To ponder

- Man's life is like a candle in the wind, or hoar-frost on the tiles. *(Chinese proverb)*
- Life is short and time is swift.
- Life means strife.

- Death surprises us in the midst of our hopes.
- Time and tide wait for no man.

To discuss

- According to this Psalm our human condition is the result of sinfulness. How far do you think this is true? What are the dangers in such a theology?
- In what ways has your life been affected by the consequences of other people's actions, and in what ways have your actions affected others?
- How far is it possible to make sense of life in terms of this world only? Is it realistic to expect happiness in this life, or must true fulfilment wait for the life to come?

To consider further

Read 2 Corinthians 4:7-5:5. Compare these words of the Apostle Paul with those of the psalmist, remembering that the latter had no concept of eternal life. Give thanks that death is not the end, but a stepping over the threshold into the everlasting arms of God.

Prayer

Living God,
    we spend so much of our lives in ceaseless striving,
    pursuing first this, then that.
We labour, we fret, we fight, we struggle,
    all our thoughts so often focused
    on present gain and immediate satisfaction.
Yet all the goals which consume us
    bring but a moment's pleasure,
    each destined to fade away.
Teach us to set our hearts first on you,
    and to discover the fulfilment you long to give us
    in both this life and the next.
Help us to live not just in the context of this brief span
    you have given here on earth,
    but in the light of your eternal purpose
    in which, by your grace, you invite us all to share.
Amen.

9 Songs of praise _____

_____ *David*

Recent years have seen a rediscovery of the place of hymns and songs within the Church. There is a bewildering variety today to choose from, with still more being added each day. Not all, of course, will stand the test of time; in fact probably precious few will. Neither will all of the traditional hymns be superseded, the words of many being too good to be discarded in favour of the latest fashion. Hopefully a balance will be found between the best of the old and the new. It is important that this should be so for, sadly, there are few areas within the Church more divisive than music – the polarisation which can develop around this never ceases to amaze me. We need to remember, as David reminds us in Psalm 98, what really counts; namely, that our songs are sung not for our own benefit but as an offering of worship to God. Whether it be a Sankey special, a Charles Wesley classic, or something more modern, ranging from Graham Kendrick to Fred Pratt Green, from Sidney Carter to a Taizé chant, what matters is that we sing to the Lord. Without that, our songs are meaningless and our time is wasted.

Reading – Psalm 98

O sing to the Lord a new song,
for he has done marvellous things.
His right hand and his holy arm
have gotten him victory.
The Lord has made known his victory;
he has revealed his vindication in the sight of the nations.

He has remembered his steadfast love and faithfulness
to the house of Israel.
All the ends of the earth have seen
the victory of our God.

Make a joyful noise to the Lord, all the earth;
break forth into joyous song and sing praises.
Sing praises to the Lord with the lyre,
with the lyre and the sound of melody.

With trumpets and the sound of the horn
make a joyful noise before the King, the Lord.

Let the sea roar, and all that fills it;
the world and those who live in it.
Let the floods clap their hands;
let the hills sing together for joy
at the presence of the Lord, for he is coming
to judge the earth.
He will judge the world with righteousness,
and the peoples with equity.

Meditation

I want to sing to the Lord –
    to lift up my voice,
    lift up my soul,
    and sing his praises to the ends of the earth!
Yes, I know that may sound a bit clichéd,
    but I don't care, for it's true –
    the love he's shown,
    the goodness,
    the mercy,
    the faithfulness not just to me but to all his people,
    too special, too wonderful for anyone to keep silent.
I want to sing from the roof-tops,
    let rip from the highest mountain!
And not just any old song,
    but something new,
    something different –
    a song which captures a little of the joy
    bubbling up within me,
    and which expresses, could it be possible,
    the majesty of our God!
It can't be done, of course –
    no words enough,
    no music sufficient to declare his greatness –
    but I'm going to try, despite that;
    I'm going to make a joyful noise,
    I'm going to pour out my heart and mind and soul,
    and I'm going to exalt the name of the Lord my God
    for all I'm worth!

Forgive me if it's not pretty, the song I sing –
    it may well not be –
    but I can promise you this:
    it will be real,
    welling up from deep within,
    a great fountain of celebration,
    irrepressible,
    inexhaustible;
    a spontaneous outpouring of praise,
    overflowing with thanksgiving,
    for he has blessed us beyond our deserving,
    he has done marvellous things for us, too many to number,
    he has heard our prayer and reached out in mercy –
    what more could anyone ask?
But enough of this,
    no time for talking;
    come join me, my friends,
    in glad and grateful worship:
    sing to the Lord a new song!

To ponder

- The music in my heart I bore, long after it was heard no more. *(William Wordsworth)*
- Words are the voice of the heart. *(Confucius)*
- Whatever is in the heart will come up to the tongue. *(Persian proverb)*
- Music has charms to soothe a savage breast. *(William Congreve)*

To discuss

- Which hymns and songs mean the most to you? Why?
- How often do you reflect on the words of hymns as you are singing them? Is there a danger sometimes of singing for the sheer enjoyment of singing? Does this matter?
- The inspiration behind David's Psalm is not simply what God has done for *him*, but what he has done for all the people of Israel. Is our worship too introspective sometimes, concerned only with how *we* are feeling? What place do hymns and songs have in ensuring a correct balance?

To consider further

Read Ephesians 5:15-20. Resolve next time you are in worship to think more deeply about the words you are singing.

Prayer

Lord,
    we thank you for the gift of song;
    for its ability to move, challenge and inspire us,
    its power to express feelings of joy and sorrow,
    hope and despair;
    its capacity to sum up our feelings
    in grateful hymns of praise.
Teach us when we worship
    to use this gift thoughtfully,
    singing to you from the heart,
    and offering not just our songs
    but ourselves with them.
Teach us to reflect on the words we use
    so that they may speak *to* us
    of all that you have done
    and speak *for* us of all *we* would do for *you*.
O Lord,
    open our lips,
    and our mouths shall declare your praise.
Amen.

10 United we stand _____

Psalmist

There are few things more sad, yet more common, than a family divided amongst itself. During the course of my ministry I've seen it over and over again – husbands who no longer speak to wives; children who have fallen out with their parents; brothers, sisters, cousins, nephews, aunts and uncles, each disowning the other and refusing to have any further dealings with them. As if that were not sad enough, frequently the cause of such bad feeling proved to be something trivial, blown up out of all proportion over the years because of an unwillingness to meet and resolve the issue. Unchecked, the poison is allowed to fester, feeding on itself rather than the original incident and destroying the lives of all concerned. Whether it was a dispute such as this or something more complex that lies behind Psalm 133, I do not know. But the reminder this simple Psalm gives of the importance of living together in harmony is one we would all do well to consider, whether at the level of our immediate family or the family of the Church. The relationships we are intended to enjoy are special; can we afford to waste them?

Reading – Psalm 133

How very good and pleasant it is
when kindred live together in unity!
It is like the precious oil on the head,
running down upon the beard,
on the beard of Aaron,
running down over the collar of his robes.
It is like the dew of Hermon,
which falls on the mountains of Zion.
For there the Lord ordained his blessing,
life for evermore.

Meditation

It was over at last,
    that foolish, futile feud,
    which had divided our family for so long,
    finally at an end,
    and what a joy it was!
We were together again,
    a family as God intended us to be,
    and the joy we felt knew no bounds.
Do you know what? –
    we hadn't spoken, some of us, for years!
Flesh and blood,
    yet we'd passed each other in the street like strangers,
    without even a glance, let alone a word.
Astonishing, isn't it!
Yet that's what it came to,
    one snub leading to another,
    insult traded for insult,
    until our pettiness bordered on the ridiculous.
Heaven knows what started it –
    we lost sight of that long ago –
    but once begun that dispute of ours took on a life of its own,
    a minor disagreement suddenly a full-blown war,
    a trivial dispute suddenly a matter of life or death.
It was pathetic,
    beyond belief,
    yet at the time we just couldn't see it,
    the whole foolish business the centre of our universe.
So day after day,
    year after year,
    we allowed it to fester on,
    until no part of life was unaffected by its poison.
What a price we paid!
When I think now of all we might have shared –
    the joys, the hopes,
    the fears, the sorrows,
    so many memories we might have built together –
    my heart aches with the tragedy of it all.
Yet there's no point brooding,
    regretting what might have been.
It's over now,
    consigned to history,
    and we're together at last,

the past behind us,
the future there for the taking,
and it's a wonderful feeling,
more special than I can ever tell you.
How good it is,
how very, very good
when kindred live together in unity.
If only we'd learned it sooner!

To ponder

- Let bygones be bygones.
- Blood is thicker than water.
- The second word makes the quarrel. *(Japanese proverb)*
- The mother of mischief is no bigger than a midge's wing.
- Broken bones well set become stronger.

To discuss

- What sort of situations bring out the worst in families? Why do you think family disputes can become so bitter?
- When does a disagreement become a feud? What sort of things can cause such an escalation? How can they be avoided?
- What do you find hardest in trying to mend a quarrel?

To consider further

Read Romans 12:14-18 and Titus 3:1-11. What do you make of Paul's advice in these letters? What lessons can we draw from these words? In what ways can they be abused?

Prayer

Lord,
    it's easy to start a quarrel,
    so much harder to end it.
It's easy to see faults in others,
    far more difficult to see them in ourselves.
It's easy to destroy relationships,
    almost impossible to build them again
    once they have been broken.
Forgive us the weaknesses
    that create divisions among us,
    separating us from our fellow human beings –
    even from our own family and friends.
Help us so far as it lies with us
    to live in harmony with all,
    and when that harmony is broken
    teach us to act as peacemakers,
    healing hurts, restoring trust
    and breaking down the barriers that come between us.
In the name of Christ,
    who shall come to reconcile all things to himself.
Amen.

11 A love that will not let us go _____

_____ *David*

For me, Psalm 139 is one of the classic texts of the Old Testament. Its verses resonate with a sense of awe as David strives to give expression to his experience of God; an experience which quite clearly has been constantly evolving, culminating in this spontaneous outpouring of praise. Few testimonies can more eloquently have summed up the wonder of God, yet according to David his words are woefully inadequate, the realities they attempt to describe ultimately beyond understanding, too wonderful for words! Do we feel a similar sense of awe before God? We may have done once, but familiarity can make us complacent, the flames which fired our faith losing something of their intensity as the years pass. David calls us to meet again with the living God whose love surrounds us, whose goodness sustains us, whose mercy astounds us and whose greatness is beyond all expression.

Reading – Psalm 139:1-18

Lord, you have searched me and known me.
You know when I sit down and when I rise up;
you discern my thoughts from far away.
You search out my path and my lying down,
and are acquainted with all my ways.
Even before a word is on my tongue,
O Lord, you know it completely.
You hem me in, behind and before,
and lay your hand upon me.
Such knowledge is too wonderful for me;
it is so high that I cannot attain it.

Where can I go from your spirit?
Or where can I flee from your presence?
If I ascend to heaven, you are there;
if I make my bed in Sheol, you are there.
If I take the wings of the morning
and settle at the farthest limits of the sea,
even there your hand shall lead me,

and your right hand shall hold me fast.
If I say, 'Surely the darkness shall cover me,
and the light around me become night,'
even the darkness is not dark to you;
the night is as bright as the day,
for darkness is as light to you.

It was you who formed my inward parts;
you knit me together in my mother's womb.
I praise you, for I am fearfully and wonderfully made.
Wonderful are your works;
that I know very well.
My frame was not hidden from you,
when I was being made in secret,
intricately woven in the depths of the earth.
Your eyes beheld my unformed substance.
In your book were written
all the days that were formed for me,
when none of them as yet existed.
How weighty to me are your thoughts, O God!
How vast is the sum of them!
I try to count them – they are more than the sand;
I come to the end – I am still with you.

Meditation

It's no good, Lord,
    it's too much for me,
    more than I can ever take in.
I've tried, you know that.
Day after day I've struggled
    to get my head round the wonder of who and what you are,
    but I just can't do it;
    your greatness is beyond the reach of human mind.
I've come far, no question,
    new insights and experiences adding to my sense of wonder,
    deepening my faith,
    enlarging my vision;
    yet I realise now that those were just a taste,
    a small sample of what is yet in store,
    for there is always more to learn,

much that is hidden still to be revealed.
It's frightening, almost,
    for you overturn all our expectations,
    at work not just in the light, but in the darkness,
    not just in the good, but in the bad –
    no place outside your purpose
    no person beyond your grace,
    your love stronger, wider, greater, deeper
    than I've even begun to imagine!
Always you are there,
    one step ahead,
    waiting to take my hand
    and lead me on to the next stage of my journey.
So that's it, Lord.
    enough is enough –
    no more tying myself into knots,
    no more juggling with the impossible.
I don't have all the answers
    and I never will have,
    but I've got you, here by my side,
    behind to guard me,
    ahead to lead me,
    above to bless me,
    within to feed me –
    your love always there,
    every moment,
    everywhere,
    in everything.
And, quite honestly, if I've got that,
    what else do I need to know!

To ponder

- The nature of God is a circle of which the centre is everywhere and the circumference is nowhere. *(Attributed to Empedocles)*
- God is the perfect poet, who in his person acts his own creations. *(Robert Browning)*
- If God did not exist, it would be necessary to invent him. *(Voltaire)*
- In youth I looked to these very skies, and probing their immensities, I found God there. *(Robert Browning)*

To discuss

- Do you find the idea of God knowing your every thought, even before you know it, an inspiring or sobering one? Why?
- David manages to keep a balance between the otherness of God and his living presence with us. Is such a balance successfully kept in the Church today?
- Have there been times when you have found God in the darkest moments of life? What were these, and in what way did you encounter God in them?
- Have you ever felt overwhelmed by the sheer wonder of God? In what kind of situations do you feel most aware of his presence?

To consider further

Read John 1:1-18. What parallels do you see between this passage and the Psalm above?

Prayer

Great and mighty God,
    we thank you that you have the power
    to constantly surprise us,
    opening up each day new horizons
    and new experiences to explore.
We can never exhaust the possibilities of life
    or the mysteries of faith.
However far we may have travelled
    along the path of discipleship,
    the journey is always only just beginning,
    such is the wonder of your grace.
Teach us to keep hold of that great truth,
    so that we may never lose our sense of awe before you.
May our hearts thrill
    as the knowledge of your loving purpose
    continues to unfold,
    this day and for evermore.
Amen.

12 Words to remember

Solomon

Since I was a boy I have always had a liking for proverbs. It is astonishing how just a few words can sum up the most profound of truths, not only encapsulating their essence but simultaneously provoking reflection about the issues these raise. A pithy saying lives on in the memory long after facts, which we have laboriously struggled to absorb, have been forgotten. No doubt this is why King Solomon similarly set such store by proverbs. He found in them a simple yet effective way of communicating the wisdom for which he was rightly famous; and in his astonishing collection which comprises the bulk of the book of Proverbs, we find an apophthegm to address just about every facet of life and faith. There is more, of course, to wisdom than simply being able to repeat such sayings parrot fashion. We need to consider what each means and, above all, to make them a part of our lives. Could we but begin to do that, we would find our insight into, and understanding of, the complex realities of daily life enriched beyond measure.

Reading – Proverbs 3:1-8

My child, do not forget my teaching,
but let your heart keep my commandments;
for length of days and years of life
and abundant welfare they will give you.

Do not let loyalty and faithfulness forsake you;
bind them around your neck,
write them on the tablet of your heart.
So you will find favour and good repute
in the sight of God and of people.

Trust in the Lord with all your heart,
and do not rely on your own insight.
In all your ways acknowledge him,
and he will make straight your paths.
Do not be wise in your own eyes;
fear the Lord, and turn away from evil.

It will be a healing for your flesh
and a refreshment for your body.

Meditation

'The fear of the Lord is the beginning of wisdom' –
    that's what my mother told me when I was just a boy,
    and I've remembered it ever since,
    a rule of thumb that's never left me.
A bit of a cliché, perhaps,
    the words in danger of tripping off the tongue
    just that bit too easily,
    but better that than for them never to stick at all.
And it can happen, believe me,
    the lesson we thought we'd learned today,
    forgotten tomorrow,
    the truth we thought we'd fathomed
    returning unexpectedly to perplex us.
Don't think you're different, for you're not.
We can all lose sight of the things that matter,
    every one of us.
Slowly but surely we start to drift,
    now this way, now that,
    drawn by hidden currents inexorably onwards
    until the shore we started from is lost to view.
I've witnessed it all too often,
    convictions quashed,
    principles compromised,
    scruples forgotten,
    as little by little the truth is eroded,
    worn down by the unrelenting tide
    of a hostile and dismissive world.
Yet it needn't be like that,
    not if you remember what really counts:
    the word of the Lord,
    the commandments he's given,
    the witness of his servants.
Make time for those,
    not just to read them but to make them part of you,
    engraved on your heart,
    inscribed in your soul,
    and you will find the way to life,

a light to guide you every step you take,
    wholeness in body, mind and spirit.
That's what my mother taught me, all those years ago,
    and that's what I've set out to teach in turn,
    to share something of the wisdom she shared with me.
Not her wisdom, you understand,
    nor mine,
    but springing from the fear of the Lord,
    sustained and nurtured by him.
Discover that, my child,
    take that lesson to heart,
    and you will find treasure indeed,
    riches beyond price.

To ponder

- A good maxim is never out of season.
- Great consolation may grow out of the smallest saying.
- Though the proverb is abandoned, it is not falsified.
- Proverbs are the children of experience.
- A proverb is the wit of one and the wisdom of many.
- Time passes away, but sayings remain.

To discuss

- How easy do you find it to keep your devotional life fresh? What aids to reflection and study do you find most helpful?
- Have there been times when it has dawned on you that your convictions have become compromised? What do you think led to such situations?
- Which pressures from society do you feel are most difficult for Christians to resist?

To consider further

Read 2 Timothy 3:14-17 and James 3:13-18. Resolve to study the Scriptures more regularly and to apply what they say to your daily life.

Prayer

Gracious God,
    you have spoken your word,
    you offer us your guidance,
    yet all too often we go astray.
Despite our desire to serve you,
    we are swayed by those around us,
    our faith undermined,
    our beliefs subtly influenced by pressures
    we are barely even aware of.
Forgive us the weakness of our commitment
    and teach us to make time for you each day
    to study your word and to reflect on your goodness.
Draw near to us
    and help us to draw near to you,
    so that you may be a part of us,
    filling us in heart and mind and soul.
In the name of Christ we ask it.
Amen.

13 Watch your tongue _____

_____ *Solomon*

Anyone who has been in an argument (and that probably means all of us) will be all too aware of the power of the tongue. As positions polarise, so words become more heated, hurled at each other in anger rather than exchanged in thoughtful debate. Tempers flare, and words give way to abuse, much said which may be regretted long afterwards. No wonder, then, that many of the proverbs of Solomon warn against the dangers of the tongue. Yet if words can be used for evil, they can equally be employed for good. Like so many of God's gifts, they are a two-edged sword, capable of being used or abused. The choice sounds straightforward enough, but the reality is very different, for words have a tendency to run away with us, developing a life of their own. Unless we learn to watch our tongues, we may well find that words become our master instead of us theirs.

Reading – Proverbs 12:6, 13-14a, 17-19; 13:2-3; 15:1-2, 4; 26:17-28

The words of the wicked are a deadly ambush,
but the speech of the upright delivers them.

The evil are ensnared by the transgression of their lips,
but the righteous escape from trouble.
From the fruit of the mouth one is filled with good things . . .

Whoever speaks the truth gives honest evidence,
but a false witness speaks deceitfully.
Rash words are like sword thrusts,
but the tongue of the wise brings healing.
Truthful lips endure for ever,
but a lying tongue lasts only a moment.

From the fruit of their words good persons eat good things,
but the desire of the treacherous is for wrongdoing.
Those who guard their mouths preserve their lives;
those who open wide their lips come to ruin.

A soft answer turns away wrath,
but a harsh word stirs up anger.

The tongue of the wise dispenses knowledge,
but the mouths of fools pour out folly . . .
A gentle tongue is a tree of life,
but perverseness in it breaks the spirit.

Like somebody who takes a passing dog by the ears
is one who meddles in the quarrel of another.
Like a maniac who shoots deadly firebrands and arrows,
so is one who deceives a neighbour
and says, 'I am only joking!'
For lack of wood the fire goes out,
and where there is no whisperer, quarrelling ceases.
As charcoal is to hot embers and wood to fire,
so is a quarrelsome person for kindling strife.
The words of a whisperer are like delicious morsels;
they go down to the inner parts of the body.
Like the glaze covering an earthen vessel
are smooth lips with an evil heart.
An enemy dissembles in speaking
while harbouring deceit within;
when an enemy speaks graciously, do not believe it,
for there are seven abominations concealed within;
though hatred is covered with guile,
the enemy's wickedness will be exposed in the assembly.
Whoever digs a pit will fall into it,
and a stone will come back on the one who starts it rolling.
A lying tongue hates its victims,
and a flattering mouth works ruin.

Meditation

Think before you speak.
It's simple advice, isn't it?
So obvious you'd hardly think it needs saying.
But it does, believe me,
    for though it may sound implausible,
    most of us do just the opposite,
    speaking first and thinking later.
Does that matter?
Well, consider for a moment the results –
    the mother wounded by a cruel jibe,
    the child crushed by a harsh rebuke,
    the marriage broken by thoughtless gossip,

the family divided by a careless remark,
each a symbol of the devastating power of words.
And there are countless more all around you, even as I speak –
a word here, a word there,
spat from curled lips,
twisted by cruel tongues,
or tossed wildly into the breeze
with no thought of the consequences –
sowing discord,
sparking hatred,
feeding bitterness.
Yet that's not the way it has to be,
for words are God's gift,
able to express so much beauty and achieve so much good.
It doesn't take much,
just a little thought and the result can be so different:
a word of thanks,
praise,
comfort,
encouragement,
spoken not to hurt but to heal,
not to curse but to bless;
offered with compassion and gentleness –
and instead of sorrow, there is joy,
instead of hatred, love,
instead of war, peace.
I've said enough,
yet more words added to those already spoken,
but promise me this,
next time you come to speak,
the words rising on your tongue,
stop and think before you say them.

To ponder

- Under the tongue men are crushed to death.
- Words have wings, and cannot be recalled.
- Better the foot slip than the tongue.
- Good words cool more than cold water.
- Least said, soonest mended.
- Flow of words is not always flow of wisdom.
- Better to remain silent and be thought a fool than to speak out and remove all doubt. (*Attributed to Abraham Lincoln*)

To discuss

- 'Sticks and stones may break my bones, but words will never hurt me.' What do you make of that proverb? Are there times when you have been hurt by words? What were they?

- Have there been times when you wanted to take back words you had spoken? Why do we say things we will regret later? What can lead us to make this mistake?

- What words have you found most helpful in your life? Are there occasions you can recall when someone has spoken the right word at the right time? What did they say?

To consider further

Read James 3:1-12. Think carefully today about the things you say. Are you in control of your tongue? Do you think before you speak? Do your words bring happiness to others, or cause hurt? Resolve to watch your tongue in the days ahead.

Prayer

Lord,
we thank you for the wonderful gift of speech,
the ability through language
to communicate with one another;
to express our thoughts and feelings;
to share information;
to move, challenge and inspire;
to offer ideas; to bring comfort.
Forgive us for the way we turn something so special
into something so ugly,
capable of causing such devastation.
Teach us to think more carefully about what we say,
and to speak always with the intention of helping
rather than hurting.
Help us to use words wisely,
in the name of Jesus Christ,
the Word made flesh.
Amen.

14 The price of idleness

Solomon

If you need a job done, ask a busy person. Words which have become a bit of a cliché, yet they are true nonetheless. For some people the very thought of hard work makes them go weak at the knees, to the point that they keep on putting it off, _ad infinitum_. Others simply get stuck in, and in no time at all the job gets done. The majority of us are probably somewhere in between. We do what's expected of us – most of the time anyway – and perhaps just occasionally, if we're feeling especially virtuous, we do that little bit extra; yet somehow there's always something left undone, just enough to niggle away in the back of the mind and disturb our peace. We know we've got to do it, but we just can't summon up the enthusiasm. We know it will have to be done eventually, yet we invariably succeed in putting it off one more day. Yet is such procrastination worth it? We may buy ourselves a little time – an evening together away from the children, a morning lie-in, an afternoon on the beach – but the thought of that job is always there, haunting us like some tantalising spectre. The longer we leave it, the worse the prospect becomes and the less we feel inclined to do it. If we are not careful, we slip into a self-perpetuating downward spiral, achieving ever less as we prevaricate all the more. The warnings of Solomon in the proverbs which follow may seem a little extreme, but beware – the danger may be more real than you think!

Reading – Proverbs 6:6-9; 13:4; 24:30-34; 26:13-16

Go to the ant, you lazybones;
consider its ways, and be wise.
Without having any chief or officer or ruler,
it prepares its food in summer,
and gathers its sustenance in harvest.
How long will you lie there, O lazybones?
When will you rise from your sleep?

The appetite of the lazy craves, and gets nothing,
while the appetite of the diligent is richly supplied.

I passed by the field of one who was lazy,
by the vineyard of a stupid person;
and see, it was all overgrown with thorns;
the ground was covered with nettles,
and its stone wall was broken down.
Then I saw and considered it;
I looked and received instruction.
A little sleep, a little slumber,
a little folding of the hands to rest,
and poverty will come upon you like a robber,
and want, like an armed warrior.

The lazy person says, 'There is a lion in the road!
There is a lion in the streets!'
As a door turns on its hinges,
so does a lazy person in bed.
The lazy person buries a hand in the dish,
and is too tired to bring it back to the mouth.
The lazy person is wiser in self-esteem
than seven who can answer discreetly.

Meditation

It's not fair, he said,
    not right;
    how could God have let it happen?
And he really meant it.
He actually believed that life had given him a raw deal,
    that his sorry plight was a twist of fate,
    and fortune had conspired against him.
No matter that he'd rested while we worked,
    that he'd made merry while we made headway –
    such details were forgotten –
    it couldn't be his fault,
    no way!
So he stood there complaining,
    bemoaning his lot,
    shaking his fist at the world.
It's hard to believe, I know,
    for it was plain enough to everyone else –
    the situation of his own making,

the inevitable result of idleness –
but he just couldn't or wouldn't see it.
You won't find many like him, thank goodness,
    not many quite so foolish or indolent,
    but I wouldn't rest on your laurels if I were you,
    for there's a little of that man in all of us,
    and perhaps rather more than you might imagine.
We've all done it, haven't we,
    postponed that job we cannot face? –
    'All in good time', we say.
    'Not today!'
    'It will keep' –
    you know the kind of thing.
And once started so it goes on . . .
    and on . . .
    and on –
    another excuse,
    another reason for delay,
    another opportunity wasted.
It's a fool's game, for you gain nothing,
    the job still there,
    weighing on your mind,
    and the longer you postpone it, the heavier it presses,
    sapping your energy more surely
    than had you faced the task.
No, take my advice and set to work,
    roll up your sleeves and get stuck in.
There'll be time to rest tomorrow,
    today's the time for action –
    it will be worth it, I assure you.

To ponder

- For the diligent the week has seven todays, for the slothful seven tomorrows.
- It is more pain to do nothing than something.
- Don't put off till tomorrow what you can do today.
- Idle folk have the least leisure.
- Idle folk lack no excuses.
- He that is busy is tempted by but one devil; he that is idle by a legion.
- Procrastination is the thief of time.

To discuss

- 'God helps those who help themselves.' How far is this old saying true? Is there a danger sometimes of expecting God to do everything for us, and forgetting our part?
- Idleness may well lead to poverty, but this doesn't mean poverty is the result of idleness. Are we sometimes guilty of assuming it is? Is this is a prevailing attitude in society today?
- What do you see as the dangers of putting something off? Can you think of illustrations from your own experience? Are there ways we can become lazy in Christian discipleship, putting off what God is asking of us? What might these be?

To consider further

Read Matthew 25:1a, 14-30; 2 Thessalonians 3:6-13; Hebrews 6:10-12. Are there areas in your life where you have become lazy? Are there areas in your Christian discipleship where you have become complacent? Resolve today to tackle that job you've been putting off, and at the same time resolve to put the gifts God has given you to good use in his service.

Prayer

Lord,
    you have given us a multitude of gifts and opportunities;
    forgive us that we sometimes fail to make use of them.
We don't think of ourselves as lazy,
    but time and again we avoid tasks
    which we ought to tackle,
    at cost to ourselves, to others
    and to you.
So many possibilities are wasted
    and so much peace of mind lost
    because we prefer to put off till tomorrow
    what we ought to do today.
Teach us to make the most of each moment,
    to utilise our talents to the full,
    and to tackle every task as it comes,
    for both our sakes and yours.
Amen.

15 The course of true love _____

_____ *Solomon*

The book of the Song of Solomon is one into which preachers seldom venture; and, if they do, the tendency is to spiritualise its message for fear of causing embarrassment to themselves or offence to their congregation. I was no exception. Let's face it, verses like 'Your rounded thighs are like jewels, the work of a master hand. Your navel is a rounded bowl that never lacks mixed wine. Your belly is a heap of wheat, encircled with lilies' (7:1-3) hardly leap out as obvious sermon texts! How to handle the book is further complicated by difficulties in identifying its true meaning. Is it, as appearances suggest, a straightforward love song, or are we intended to see in its imagery allusions to God's relationship with his people Israel? For years the latter interpretation was the preferred option, but scholars today seem pretty much in agreement that the Song of Solomon is above all a celebration of human love. The language may seem flowery and over-sentimental at times – almost, you might say, an Old Testament Mills and Boon! – but in these days of sexual promiscuity and marital breakdown it is worth reflecting on the joys, and also the limitations, of physical relationships.

Reading – Song of Solomon 4:1-7

How beautiful you are, my love,
how very beautiful!
Your eyes are doves behind your veil.
Your hair is like a flock of goats,
moving down the slopes of Gilead.
Your teeth are like a flock of shorn ewes
that have come up from the washing,
all of which bear twins,
and not one among them is bereaved.
Your lips are like a crimson thread,
and your mouth is lovely.
Your cheeks are like halves of a pomegranate
behind your veil.
Your neck is like the tower of David,
built in courses;
on it hang a thousand bucklers,

all of them shields of warriors.
Your two breasts are like two fawns,
twins of a gazelle,
that feed among the lilies.
Until the day breathes and the shadows flee,
I will hasten to the mountain of myrrh
and the hill of frankincense.
You are altogether beautiful, my love;
there is no flaw in you.

Meditation

My rose without a thorn, that's how I saw her,
    beautiful beyond measure,
    lovelier than the morning dew.
I thrilled when I heard her voice,
    shivered with joy when I saw her face,
    and when I held her close,
    our limbs entwined,
    our bodies as one,
    my heart leapt within me.
She was everything a man could have wanted –
    attractive,
    sensual,
    passionate,
    her eyes as blue as topaz,
    lips sweet as honey,
    skin soft as down.
No wonder that I loved her,
    more fiercely and passionately
    than I thought myself capable of.
It changed, of course;
    well, it had to, didn't it?
She had her flaws after all, just as I do,
    and we had our moments as the years went by –
    harsh words,
    angry exchanges,
    even the occasional fall out –
    love tested to the limit.
Yet she's still special,
    as precious to me now as the day we met,
    if not more.

We've moved on, undeniably,
  slowly,
  almost imperceptibly,
  our relationship evolving –
  the flame of desire not so strong, though still burning,
  the expressions of affection not so obvious,
  yet we are closer than we've ever been,
  welded together through everything we've shared –
  a union not just of body, but also mind and spirit.
I loved her then, more than I believed possible.
I love her now, more than ever.
And I'll go on doing so, just as I promised,
  until my dying day,
  until death us do part.

To ponder

- Love is a flower which turns into a fruit at marriage.
- The course of true love never did run smooth. *(William Shakespeare)*
- Marriage must constantly vanquish a monster that devours everything; the monster of habit. *(Honoré de Balzac)*
- Love is a fair garden and marriage a field of nettles.
- Where there's marriage without love, there will be love without marriage.

To discuss

- A good relationship must be worked at, but does this guarantee every relationship can be saved? Is it right to continue with a loveless relationship, or does the time come when it is right to end it? Does the Church's attitude on marriage and sexual relationships help or hinder?
- Recent years have seen a growing openness about sex and an increase in sex education, to the point that some feel it has gone too far. What are the dangers of such openness and what are the advantages?
- What are the essential ingredients of a fulfilling relationship? What sort of pressures tend to undermine these? Is there any way of preventing relationships from becoming stale and losing their sparkle?

To consider further

Read Ephesians 5:22-33. Like all biblical passages on the subject of marriage, these verses reflect the prevailing attitude at the time towards women. Few women today, in my view quite rightly, are willing to pledge obedience to their husbands. What lessons can nonetheless be drawn from this passage?

Prayer

Gracious God,
    we thank you for the gift of human love
    and for the joy that this can bring.
We thank you for the love we are able to give and receive,
    and for the fulfilment that comes from a union
    of body, mind and spirit.
Reach out to all those whose love has been broken,
    those who have lost loved ones
    and those whose love has grown cold.
Restore love in these lives,
    and deepen that in our own,
    so that the love we are privileged to share
    may grow and flourish every step of our journey together.
In the name of Christ.
Amen.

16 The road to nowhere

The Teacher

Few books in the Bible come as more of a surprise than the book of Ecclesiastes. The opening few words, after introductory preliminaries, unmistakably set the scene for all that is to follow: 'Vanity of vanities, says the Teacher, vanity of vanities! All is vanity.' Quite simply, this isn't the sort of message you expect to find in the pages of Scripture, but, as you read on, it gets worse! How about this, for example: 'What do mortals get from all the toil and strain with which they toil under the sun? For all their days are full of pain, and their work is a vexation; even at night their minds do not rest. This also is vanity.' And so it goes on, in similar vein, page after page. There are some who find this apparent world-weariness a little shocking, others who simply don't know what to make of it. Personally, I find here a refreshing honesty about life, as the Teacher voices inner frustrations and deeply held feelings which most of us are reluctant to acknowledge, let alone tackle. Perhaps the note of cynicism finally goes too far, but the issues raised nonetheless need to be faced. Tackle them squarely, and I believe our faith will grow stronger, able to face the vicissitudes of life and make sense of the purposes of God within them.

Reading – Ecclesiastes 1:2-11

Vanity of vanities, says the Teacher,
vanity of vanities! All is vanity.
What do people gain from all the toil
at which they toil under the sun?
A generation goes, and a generation comes,
but the earth remains for ever.
The sun rises and the sun goes down,
and hurries to the place where it rises.
The wind blows to the south,
and goes around to the north;
round and round goes the wind,
and on its circuits the wind returns.
All streams run to the sea,
but the sea is not full;
to the place where the streams flow,

there they continue to flow.
All things are wearisome;
more than one can express;
the eye is not satisfied with seeing,
or the ear filled with hearing.
What has been is what will be,
and what has been done is what will be done;
there is nothing new under the sun.
Is there a thing of which it is said,
'See, this is new'?
It has already been, in the ages before us.
The people of long ago are not remembered,
nor will there be any remembrance
of people yet to come
by those who come after them.

Meditation

I dared to dream once – can you believe that?
It may seem incredible now,
    but there was a time, not so long ago,
    when I was a hopeless, headstrong romantic,
    bursting with plans to change the world!
An angry young man, that's what they called me,
    and if one or two felt I went a bit too far,
    even branding me a rebel,
    the majority applauded my ideals,
    a welcome oasis in a parched and shrivelled land.
How things change –
    they wouldn't recognise me now!
Not that I look so different outwardly,
    but, inside, I'm a shadow of my former self,
    battered,
    bruised,
    beaten.
It's not been a conscious thing,
    principles compromised for the sake of expediency.
Quite the opposite –
    I still long to blaze with the same enthusiasm –
    to feel the pulse quicken,
    heart race,
    imagination soar –

but I can't,
and somehow I don't think I ever will again.
You see, I've seen people come and people go,
life ebb and flow like the seasons;
I've seen promises made and promises broken,
hopes raised, then turned to dust;
I've seen joy today become sorrow tomorrow,
pleasure one moment bring pain the next;
and it's finally worn me down,
no point, no meaning, left in anything.
There *is* more, of course, I know that,
for whether I see it or not,
God is working in this strange old world of ours;
and, yes, one day those long-gone dreams of mine
will come true –
a new beginning,
new kingdom,
new life.
But until that time comes, my advice to you is simple:
enjoy yourself by all means,
make the most of what you have,
but don't get carried away,
and, above all, don't put all your eggs in one basket,
for believe me, it's just not worth it.

To ponder

- The world is a net, the more we stir in it, the more we are entangled.
- The world is a ladder for some to go up and some to go down.
- The world is like a dancing girl – it dances for a little while to everyone. (*Arabic proverb*)
- It will all be the same a hundred years from now.
- The life of man is a winter's day and a winter's way.

To discuss

- Do you think a degree of scepticism, even cynicism, about life is a good or a bad thing? Why?
- The Teacher appears to see little of merit in this life? How far does this square with the Christian faith? Does it reinforce or contradict it?

- How would you respond to someone for whom life has lost its sparkle?

To consider further

Read 1 John 2:15-17. In what sense is it wrong for Christians to love this world? In what sense is it right?

Prayer

Gracious God,
    we bring to you today our frustrated hopes,
    our broken dreams and battered expectations.
As the years pass,
    though some of our visions for the future are realised,
    many are not and probably never will be.
Our ideals are replaced by a world-weary cynicism,
    a sense that we've seen it all before.
We become reconciled to what is
    rather than hunger for what yet might be.
Teach us to accept when such realism is necessary,
    but teach us also still to believe in your purpose
    and your ability to change the world.
Teach us to trust in your transforming power,
    for you alone can make all things new.
Amen.

17 A time for everything _____

_____ *The Teacher*

If the theme of Ecclesiastes seems generally to be one of almost total negativity, there is nonetheless a glimmer of light at the end of the tunnel. Not, it must be said, a sudden about-face, nor indeed any indication that the Teacher has moderated his views about the futility of life, but an acknowledgement that one thing at least can make sense of it all, and that is God. The end of the matter, he tells us, is this: 'Fear God, and keep his commandments; for that is the whole duty of everyone.' Hardly an outpouring of praise, still less suggesting any sense of celebration, but in these sombre, even stern, words of conclusion, we are offered, after all the apparent hopelessness that has gone before, reason to hope. Exactly what went through the Teacher's mind as he summed up his arguments I have no idea, but I like to believe he discovered a new sense of purpose, a renewed awareness of God which breathed unexpected joy into his life. Of course, this is only speculation, and unfounded speculation at that; not so much a reading between the lines as a rewriting of the script. Yet there is just something about the note on which the book ends to make me feel that alongside the cynicism of all that goes before there is a wry smile, a shrug of the shoulders and a spark of anticipation spluttering back into life.

Reading – Ecclesiastes 11:8-12:7

Even those who live many years shall rejoice in them all; yet let them remember that the days of darkness will be many. All that comes is vanity.

Rejoice, young man, while you are young, and let your heart cheer you in the days of your youth. Follow the inclination of your heart and the desire of your eyes, but know that for all these things God will bring you into judgement.

Banish anxiety from your mind, and put away pain from body; for youth and the dawn of life are vanity.

Remember your creator in the days of your youth, before the days of trouble come, and the years draw near when you will say, 'I have no pleasure in them'; before the sun and the light and the moon and the stars are darkened and the clouds return with the rain; in the day when the guards of the house tremble, and the strong men are bent, and the women who grind cease working because they are few, and those who look through the windows see dimly; when the doors on the street are shut, and the sound of the grinding is low, and one rises up at the sound of the bird, and all the daughters of song are brought low; when one is afraid of heights, and terrors are in the road: the almond tree blossoms, the grasshopper drags itself along and desire fails; because all must go to their eternal home, and the mourners will go about the streets; before the silver cord is snapped, and the golden bowl is broken, and the pitcher is broken at the fountain, and the wheel broken at the cistern, and the dust returns to the earth as it was, and the breath returns to God who gave it. Vanity of vanities, says the Teacher; all is vanity.

Meditation

They think me wise, some people –
    can you believe that?
They actually hold me up as an example
    of insight, understanding and discernment.
Well, more fool them!
Oh, I've learned a bit *now,* I grant you;
    the harsh lessons of experience have finally sunk home,
    and if you call that wisdom, then I can't argue.
But it took me long enough, didn't it? –
    too long by half,
    so you won't catch me blowing my own trumpet,
    I can assure you!
I've been a fool, that's how I see it,
    for I've frittered away the years in an empty and futile search,
    brooding first over this, then about that:
    the injustices of life,
    the riddle of death,
    the search for joy,
    the bearing of sorrow,
    the lure of wealth,
    the plight of the poor –
    you name it, I've pondered it,
    hour upon hour,
    year after year,
    my life's work to scale the heights and plumb the depths.
Yet look where it's got me –
    disillusioned,
    disheartened,
    dismayed –
    the world, for all its beauty, meaningless,

a chasing after the wind.
Is that the last word?
It can't be,
    for I realise now I got the balance wrong,
    too full of self,
    too short on God;
    too full of my own ideas to respond to his guidance.
I should have stopped long ago,
    made time when I was still young,
    life before me,
    to pause and listen to his voice,
    but I thought I could go it alone,
    find by myself the answers I sought.
It wasn't the searching that was wrong, don't think that –
    there's a time for that as there's a time for everything –
    but I lost my bearings,
    in my search for knowledge and understanding
    letting life slip through my fingers.
I could brood about *that* now, all too easily,
    the opportunities I've missed,
    the days I've wasted,
    but not this time.
I may not be quite the man I was –
    the years have taken their toll –
    but I know now what really matters,
    and I'm going to savour the time that's left to me,
    every day,
    every moment,
    celebrating each one as the gift of my creator.
And if you would be wise, my friend,
    then you will do the same,
    not putting it off till tomorrow but starting today,
    here and now.
Do that, and you won't go far wrong!

To ponder

- This world is nothing, except it tend to another.
- The world is too much with us; late and soon, getting and spending
we lay waste our powers. *(William Wordsworth)*
- What is this world if, full of care, we have no time to stand and stare?
(W. H. Davies)

- Life is half spent before we know what it is.
- Good counsel never comes amiss.
- If you wish good advice, consult an old man.

To discuss

- Have you, like the Teacher, ever felt a sense of the emptiness of life? When, and why?
- What things give most meaning to life for you? How secure are these? What would it take to shake them?
- Do you think we give more thought to spiritual values as we grow older, or less?

To consider further

Read Matthew 6:25-34. Are we too preoccupied sometimes with things which cannot satisfy, rather than the things of God which alone can meet our deepest needs?

Prayer

Eternal God,
    we spend so much of our lives seeking happiness,
    yet much of the time we are frustrated.
We turn from one thing to another,
    believing for a moment
    that it may offer the fulfilment that we crave,
    but so many pleasures are fleeting,
    here today and gone tomorrow.
There are times when life seems empty,
    when nothing seems permanent,
    not even those things most precious to us.
Help us to find the rest for our souls
    which you alone can give;
    to discover in you that inner peace which can never change
    but will go on satisfying for all eternity.
Help us to live each day in tune with you,
    rejoicing in all you have given
    and anticipating all you have yet to give.
Through Christ our Lord.
Amen.

18 God is able!

Shadrach, Meshach and Abednego

The story of Shadrach, Meshach and Abednego is one of the great biblical classics, an unforgettable tale of courage and the triumph of good over evil which has captured the hearts of countless generations. But, as with all classics, there is a danger that familiarity may inure us to the full impact of the underlying message. We read the story, knowing the final outcome of events – for Shadrach, Meshach and Abednego there was no such luxury. They staked all in the faith that God would deliver them. They risked death itself rather than compromise their convictions. They had no doubt God could save them if he wished; whether he would choose to do so was another matter.

Reading – Daniel 3:1, 3-6, 8-9, 12-14, 16-18

King Nebuchadnezzar made a golden statue whose height was sixty cubits and whose width was six cubits; he set it up on the plain of Dura in the province of Babylon.

So the satraps, the prefects, and the governors, the counsellors, the treasurers, the justices, the magistrates, and all the officials of the provinces, assembled for the dedication of the statue that King Nebuchadnezzar had set up. When they were standing before the statue that Nebuchadnezzar had set up, the herald proclaimed aloud, 'You are commanded, O peoples, nations, and languages, that when you hear the sound of the horn, pipe, lyre, trigon, harp, drum, and entire musical ensemble, you are to fall down and worship the golden statue that King Nebuchadnezzar has set up. Whoever does not fall down and worship shall immediately be thrown into a furnace of blazing fire.'

Accordingly, at this time certain Chaldeans came forward and denounced the Jews. They said to King Nebuchadnezzar, 'O king, live for ever! . . . There are certain Jews whom you have appointed over the affairs of the province of Babylon: Shadrach, Meshach, and Abednego. These pay no heed to you, O king. They do not serve your gods and they do not worship the golden statue that you have set up.'

Then Nebuchadnezzar in furious rage commanded that Shadrach, Meshach and Abednego be brought in; so they brought those men before the king. Nebuchadnezzar said to them, 'Is it true, O Shadrach, Meshach, and Abednego, that you do not serve my gods and you do not worship the golden statue that I have set up?'

Shadrach, Meshach and Abednego answered the king, 'O Nebuchadnezzar, we have no need to present a defence to you in this matter. If our God whom we serve is able to deliver us from the furnace of blazing fire and out of your hand, O king, let him deliver us. But if not, be it known to you, O king, that we will not serve your gods and we will not worship the golden statue that you have set up.'

Meditation

Did we know God would save us,
    that whatever we faced he would see us through,
    safe to the other side?
Well, no, we didn't actually,
    despite what some may tell you.
We wish we had done,
    for we'd have felt a whole lot happier,
    ready to take whatever the king might throw at us.
But there were no guarantees, no cast-iron certainties –
    we had to wait, and trust, and hope.
Of course he *could* deliver us,
    but *would* he?
Who could say?
After all, why bother with us?
We were nobody special,
    just three young men from Judah,
    and though Nebuchadnezzar had singled us out
    for special treatment,
    it didn't mean God had done the same.
We wouldn't be the first people to die for their faith, nor the last.
Yet at the time that wasn't our chief concern –
    our faith was on the line,
    our freedom, our integrity, our identity as a nation
    hanging in the balance,
    and we had the chance to tip the scales.
It wouldn't have taken much to toe the line,
    just a quick bow and it would all have been over –
    surely not too awful a pill to swallow?
But what then,
    what would happen the next time, and the time after,
    when the challenge came again?
First one compromise, then another,
    and before long there'd be nothing left,
    our lives bought at the cost of our souls.

So we stood firm,
    hoping when it came to it he'd see reason,
    respect our consciences,
    honour our principles,
    but we were wrong,
    not even a glimmer of compassion as he sent us off to our deaths.
I can't describe the heat of that furnace,
    enough to knock you over before you even got close,
    and as they thrust us towards it, our blood ran cold,
    limbs frozen in abject terror,
    as hope began to fade.
There was still time, of course,
    time for God to step in and save us –
    a last-minute reprieve,
    a stay of execution.
We knew he *could* do it, but *would* he?
And then they opened the door and hurled us in,
    guards collapsing in agony as the heat overwhelmed them,
    and we thought it was all over,
    three more martyrs, soon forgotten.
Only it wasn't three,
    there were four of us, and we were alive,
    walking unharmed in the fire,
    not even a hair on our heads singed by flames.
You think Nebuchadnezzar was puzzled by what he saw?
He wasn't the only one!
But then the truth dawned,
    as our words came back to us:
    'Our God is able to deliver us from the fiery furnace.'
That's what we'd claimed,
    that's what we hoped,
    and that's what we found.
We knew he *could* do it –
    we knew now he *had*!

To ponder

- Courage and resolution are the spirit and soul of virtue.
- Great things are done more through courage than through wisdom.
- To a brave and faithful man, nothing is difficult.
- Where God will help, nothing does harm.
- Nothing is impossible to a willing heart.

To discuss

- What arguments could Shadrach, Meshach and Abednego have come up with to justify kneeling before Nebuchadnezzar's image? How would you have acted in their place?
- Have there been times when God has acted for you in situations which you felt to be hopeless? What were they and in what way did God help?
- Shadrach, Meshach and Abednego, like Daniel, were delivered from danger by God, but faith doesn't guarantee such deliverance. Many over the years have been martyred for their beliefs. What are the implications of this for 'having faith'? Are we open to the possibility that God's will may not coincide with ours?

To consider further

Read Ephesians 6:10-17. How 'strong in the Lord' would *we* be if our faith was put to the test?

Prayer

Sovereign God,
    we thank you for those who have had the courage
    to stand up for their faith
    in the face of persecution and danger,
    those whose dedication to you
    has been an inspiration and example to others.
We thank you that today we are free to worship as we please,
    without any need for fear or secrecy.
But, above all, we thank you for the assurance
    that whatever we may face,
    whatever dangers may threaten us,
    you are able to deliver us from evil.
In life and in death you are by our side,
    so that finally nothing will be able to separate us
    from the wonder of your love.
Help us, then, to offer you our heartfelt worship,
    and to honour you each day with faithful service,
    to the glory of your name.
Amen.

19 The disturbing truth _____

_____ *Daniel*

'Tell me truthfully, what do you think?' How often have you been asked
that? And how often, concealing your embarrassment and avoiding
the questioner's eyes, have you proceeded to offer at best a half-truth
and at worst a downright lie? The truth, the whole truth and nothing
but the truth may be an ultimate goal in the eyes of the law; in the
daily business of human relationships it is often something we shy
away from for fear of hurting others or reflecting badly on ourselves.
To tell somebody what they'd rather not hear takes courage, especially
when the result is to place us firmly in the firing line. A little white lie
can seem the most attractive option for all concerned. Yet where
would we be today without those who have had the courage to speak
out in the cause of truth, regardless of the consequences? The thought
scarcely bears thinking about. Of course there are some situations when
honesty needs to be tempered with sensitivity, but we must beware of
using this as an excuse for shirking important issues – moral cowardice
can easily become a habit. Truth may sometimes be painful; we all nevertheless need to face it.

Reading – Daniel 5:1-9, 13a, 16b-17, 23-31

King Belshazzar made a great festival for a thousand of his lords, and
he was drinking wine in the presence of the thousand. Under the
influence of the wine, Belshazzar commanded that they bring in the
vessels of gold and silver that his father Nebuchadnezzar had taken
out of the temple in Jerusalem, so that the king and his lords, his
wives, and his concubines might drink from them. So they brought in
the vessels of gold and silver that had been taken out of the temple,
the house of God in Jerusalem, and the king and his lords, his wives,
and his concubines drank from them. They drank the wine and
praised the gods of gold and silver, bronze, iron, wood and stone.
  Immediately the fingers of a human hand appeared and began
writing on the plaster of the wall of the royal palace, next to the lamp-
stand. The king was watching the hand as it wrote. Then the king's
face turned pale, and his thoughts terrified him. His limbs gave way,
and his knees knocked together. The king cried aloud to bring in the
enchanters, the Chaldeans, and the diviners; and the king said to the
wise men of Babylon, 'Whoever can read this writing and tell me its

interpretation shall be clothed in purple, have a chain of gold around his neck, and rank third in the kingdom.' Then all the king's wise men came in, but they could not read the writing or tell the king the interpretation. Then King Belshazzar became greatly terrified and his face turned pale, and his lords were perplexed.

Then Daniel was brought in before the king. The king said to Daniel, 'If you are able to read the writing and tell me its interpretation, you shall be clothed in purple, have a chain of gold around your neck, and rank third in the kingdom.'

Then Daniel answered in the presence of the king, 'Let your gifts be for yourself, or give your rewards to someone else. Nevertheless I will read the writing to the king and let him know the interpretation. . . . You have exalted yourself against the Lord of heaven! The vessels of his temple have been brought in before you, and you and your lords and your concubines have been drinking wine from them. You have praised the gods of silver and gold, of bronze, iron, wood, and stone, which do not see or hear or know; but the God in whose power is your very breath, and to whom you belong in all your ways, you have not honoured. So from his presence the hand was sent and this writing was inscribed. And this is the writing that was inscribed: MENE, MENE, TEKEL, and PARSIN. This is the interpretation of the matter: MENE, God has numbered the days of your kingdom and brought it to an end; TEKEL, you have been weighed on the scales and found wanting; PERES, your kingdom is divided and given to the Medes and Persians.'

Then Belshazzar gave the command, and Daniel was clothed in purple, a chain of gold was put around his neck, and a proclamation was made concerning him that he should rank third in the kingdom.

That very night Belshazzar, the Chaldean king, was killed. And Darius the Mede received the kingdom, being about sixty-two years old.

Meditation

I knew what it meant immediately,
    the moment I saw the writing on the wall,
    but could I tell it,
    dare I pronounce the fateful words?
It was a tough decision, I can tell you,
    for who was I,
    a mere exile from the land of Judah,
    to stand before the king of Babylon and declare God's judgement –
    the end of his reign,
    the collapse of his kingdom?
Whatever else, I would hardly be popular,

lucky, more like, to escape with my life.
Yet when the question came there was no hesitation,
    no doubt in my mind,
    the issue confronting me suddenly crystal clear.
He'd laughed in the face of God for too long, that man,
    strutting about like some preening peacock,
    as if he were lord not just of Babylon, but the whole world.
And if that wasn't enough, worse had followed,
    not just pride but sacrilege –
    our holy vessels plundered from the temple,
    desecrated for some drunken orgy,
    all so that he could make merry with his cronies.
A huge joke, he considered it,
    the most fun he'd had in ages,
    and proof conclusive that nothing and no one
    could compare with the mighty Belshazzar,
    ruler of the greatest empire the world had so far seen.
Well, he was in for a rude awakening,
    for he'd gone too far this time,
    even God's patience tested beyond the limit.
And that's what I told him, straight down the line.
No beating about the bush,
    no dressing up the truth,
    but the bare and simple facts –
    his time had come,
    the party was over,
    the day of reckoning was at hand.
It had to be said,
    and I was glad to say it,
    but I waited afterwards with bated breath,
    expecting at any moment to feel the full force of his fury.
Yet to the man's credit, it never came.
He just nodded quietly, with an air of resignation,
    almost as if he'd known what was coming,
    his worst fears confirmed,
    ready to bow at last to something higher than himself.
It wasn't the message he wanted to hear,
    hardly one to welcome,
    but he recognised it for what it was,
    the truth, pure and simple,
    and it won respect,
    a grudging admiration,
    even from him.

To ponder

- Truth's best ornament is nakedness.
- All truths are not to be told.
- No one was ever ruined by speaking the truth. *(Hindi proverb)*
- He who speaks the truth must have one foot in the stirrup.

To discuss

- Have there been situations in which you have felt a half-truth was justified? What were these? Have there been times when you have ducked the truth, even though you know you should have spoken it? Why did you act as you did?
- How do we respond to criticism? What is our automatic reaction? Are we open to the possibility that it may be justified?
- We live in an age of spin-doctoring, society reconciled to the idea of people being economical with the truth and accustomed to the best gloss being put on to unpalatable facts. What are the long-term effects and implications of this? How far are these equally applicable to our own lives?

To consider further

Read Acts 7:51-60. The fate of Stephen reminds us that the truth is by no means always welcome. Are we prepared for the hostility we might face in turn?

Prayer

Loving God,
    we claim to be seekers after truth,
    but the reality is that it sometimes scares us.
It probes too deeply into areas we prefer kept hidden;
    it challenges us in ways we would rather not face;
    it exposes issues we find hard to deal with.
Despite our fine-sounding words
    we are often less than honest with ourselves
    and with others.
Forgive us,
    and give us the courage and sensitivity we need
    both to face the truth and to speak it,
    in the name of Christ,
    the way, the truth, and the life.
Amen.

20 The courage of our convictions _____

_____ *Daniel*

The story of Daniel in the lions' den must be one of the best known in the whole of the Old Testament – a tale which has been told and retold across the centuries, delighting countless generations. It is a classic example of good conquering evil, a victory against all the odds. But, of course, it needed the faith and courage of Daniel for that triumph to happen, his willingness to make a stand for the things he believed in, never mind the consequences. Today, thankfully, times are very different; there is little chance of us being fed to the lions, not literally anyway! But we need people of Daniel's stature as much as ever; people ready to risk all in the cause of truth, ready to hold firmly to their principles despite every attempt to sway them. Have we even a fraction of that courage and commitment?

Reading – Daniel 6:6-11

The presidents and satraps conspired and came to the king and said to him, 'O King Darius, live for ever! All the presidents of the kingdom, the prefects and the satraps, the counsellors and the governors are agreed that the king should establish an ordinance and enforce an interdict, that whoever prays to anyone, divine or human, for thirty days, except to you, O king, shall be thrown into a den of lions. Now, O king, establish the interdict and sign the document, so that it cannot be changed, according to the law of the Medes and the Persians, which cannot be revoked.' Therefore King Darius signed the document and interdict.

Although Daniel knew that the document had been signed, he continued to go to his house, which had windows in its upper room open towards Jerusalem, and to get down on his knees three times a day to pray to his God and praise him, just as he had done previously. The conspirators came and found Daniel praying and seeking mercy before his God.

Meditation

I knew it was a trap, the moment they announced it –
    I'd have been a fool not to, wouldn't I? –
    and, believe me, I was under no illusions
    as to the inevitable outcome.

It had been coming for a long time –
    jealousy turning to resentment,
    and resentment to hatred –
    so, when the news broke
    the writing, so to speak, was on the wall.
This was it:
    they were out to destroy me,
    to put paid to my faith once and for all.
Was I scared?
Of course I was –
    beside myself with terror!
It just didn't bear thinking about –
    flesh ripped to shreds,
    limb torn from limb,
    a ghastly, grisly death.
So why did I carry on regardless, I hear you ask?
Couldn't I at least have been a touch more discreet,
    a shade less provocative? –
    no one would have blamed me.
And you're right, it's what the king said himself.
Had I only gone to another room,
    or simply drawn the curtains,
    it would have saved so much unnecessary trouble.
But would it?
Even supposing my enemies had been satisfied,
    happy to have compromised my convictions,
    could that have been a happy ending?
I don't think so.
You see, it wasn't only about me,
    it was about my people –
    our freedom, our future, our faith –
    and had I given in on that one point,
    who could say what might have followed?
It could have spelt all manner of persecution for us all.
So I went up to my room as usual,
    and knelt in prayer,
    making quite certain nobody could miss me.
It was purgatory, every moment,
    the hardest prayer of my life,
    and, I have to confess,
    if I had one eye on God
    the other was on that pit of lions,
    and the picture before me was far from pretty.

Yet when the moment came
    and I was thrown among them,
    what a surprise,
    a miracle if ever there was one!
They were like kittens,
    more interested in play than prey!
The Lord had honoured my faith and closed their mouths!
You think me brave?
Well, perhaps a little,
    though I tell you what –
    there's a sense in which it was *easy* for me,
    for I knew what I was up against,
    the threat I was facing,
    the issues involved.
It's the unseen pressures which frighten me,
    the slow, subtle manipulation,
    the erosion of faith by stealth,
    that's what I'm not sure I could cope with, even now.
And, make no mistake, it's not just me
    who might face *that* den of lions,
    it's all of us.
May God deliver us from the time of trial!

Reading – Daniel 6:19-23

Then, at break of day, the king got up and hurried to the den of lions. When he came near the den where Daniel was, he cried out anxiously to Daniel, 'O Daniel, servant of the living God, has your God whom you faithfully serve been able to deliver you from the lions?' Daniel then said to the king, 'O king, live for ever! My God sent his angel and shut the lions' mouths so that they would not hurt me, because I was found blameless before him; and also before you, O king, I have done no wrong.' Then the king was exceedingly glad and commanded that Daniel be taken up out of the den, and no kind of harm was found on him, because he had trusted his God.

To ponder

- Truth is mighty and will prevail.
- Truth may walk through the world unarmed. *(Arabic proverb)*
- The longer you look at it the less you will like it.
- Fear can keep a man out of danger, but courage can support him through it.
- In things that must be it is good to be resolute.

To discuss

- Would you have followed the course Daniel took after the decree of Darius was signed, or would you have looked for a compromise solution? What reasons can you give to justify the latter? Why do you think Daniel chose the path he did?

- Are there more subtle pressures on us today to compromise our beliefs? What are they, and what is the best way to meet them?

- Daniel made a public stand for his faith, but this may not always be appropriate. Christians in the early days of the Christian Church worshipped in the catacombs of Rome, and used the sign of the fish as a sort of secret code to indicate their faith to those in the know. Should they have faced the Roman authorities head on, or was their course of action right as well as understandable?

To consider further

Read Matthew 24:9-14. Pray for those who are persecuted today for their faith, and resolve to make more of the freedom you have to share your faith openly with others.

Prayer

Lord,
    we thank you for the privilege we have
    of being able to worship and witness to you freely.
We thank you that we can read your word
    and declare your name
    without fear of recrimination.
Yet save us from ever imagining because of this
    that our faith is safe from challenge.
We live in a world in which Christian values
    are constantly being undermined,
    where greed and selfishness are held up as virtues,
    where wealth and success have all too often replaced you
    as the real object of humankind's devotion.
And every day the pressure is there to conform;
    to give a little ground – first here, then there,
    until little by little our convictions are diluted
    and the distinctiveness of our faith destroyed.
Teach us to be awake to the dangers we face,
    and give us strength to resist them
    if we hold fast to you.
Amen.

Final prayer

Living God,
    for all the times we have wrestled against you,
    flouting your will,
    ignoring your call,
    disobeying your commandments,
    resisting your guidance,
    forgive us.

In all the times we wrestle with you,
    striving to understand more,
    searching for meaning,
    grappling with our unbelief,
    begging for your help,
    hear us.

In all the times we wrestle in faith,
    seeking to do your will,
    working towards your kingdom,
    committing ourselves to your service,
    confronting evil and injustice in your name,
    bless us.

Teach us not to contend *against* you
    but to work *with* you,
    to grapple earnestly with the great mysteries of faith,
    and to give of ourselves freely in the cause of Christ.

Go with us we pray,
    and may your word live within us,
    a lamp for our path
    and a fire on our tongue,
    to the glory of your name.
Amen.

Index of Bible passages _____

(References are to meditation rather than page numbers)

Index of principal characters _____

(References are to meditation rather than page numbers)

Index of principal themes _____

(References are to meditation rather than page numbers)